Awaken Yourself

Book 1

CRISTINA JOY

Awaken Yourself

Book One

Step by step guide to happiness

Silence the noise and awaken the joy
of being alive

London, 2021

ISBN: 9798751118747
Affirmations and personal development podcasts on Youtube:
https://www.youtube.com/channel/UCHBJw6KuIi9nz8V59S6tlcg

Book a free 1-1 coaching session and get ready to breakthrough your limitations.
cristina@joyacademyglobal.com

Let's connect on social media:

Facebook: @cristinajoyglobal   Instagram: @cristinajoyglobal

CRISTINA JOY

www.joyacademyglobal.com
cristina@joyacademyglobal.com

A note from Joy

This book is dedicated to YOU.
You, who are attracted to remember.
To you, who thinks life is more than you see.
To you, who believes life is meant to be enjoyed.
To you, who know that well-being is your birth right.
You, who are looking for your own truth and light.

To YOU:

Beautiful soul, I'm glad this book found you.
The reason why you are on your journey to awaken from the
illusion of suffering to happiness is because you are tired of
accepting, as truths, things that insult your soul.
I honour you for being here.
My deepest intention in everything I write, say and do is to
awaken humanity to the inner joy that is waiting to come to
life.
To do this, I awakened the joy in me.
My strongest purpose is to eliminate all suffering in the
world, therefore, I am eliminating all that is negative in me
and my desire is to inspire you to do the same. By eliminating
all that is negative in us, we are paving a new path of light for
ourselves and those around us.
The greatest gift you can give to the world is that of your
own transformation.

We change the world, by becoming better people.
Thank you for doing your part.
Release any expectations and just enjoy the journey.

I love you!

Introduction

It was 7/11/2020, 11:11 p.m. I was in the eighth month of a global pandemic, in lockdown, at home, in London.

After a full day of "working from home", my eyes closed in front of my laptop, while I was looking for a way to alleviate the global suffering, to help as many people as possible to get through these times more easily. No matter how tired my eyes were, they somehow noticed that it was 11:11 and I smiled. It is said that 11:11 is a divine sign of synchronicity, and that when you see these numbers, you are aligned with the Universe. At that moment, my soul sparkled and I felt an intuition like I had never felt before.

I opened a word file and started typing: 7 Books, Awaken Yourself. Book 1 is published on 11/11/2020.

I stopped confused. I've written books before, but I've never felt inspired to publish them. Everything seemed so clear and certain that I could not believe it. With a trace of doubt though, I was wondering how the hell the first book would be ready on 11/11/2020? There were only 4 days until then. The doubt lasted less than a minute, as my fingers began to type the first chapter. I completely lost track of time. My fingers continued to type non-stop, with a "flow" difficult to describe in words. I was definitely "in the zone". It wasn't long before the second chapter was ready. When I lifted my fingers from the keyboard, it was 11:11 in the morning. I had written for 12 hours non-stop and I felt fresh, as if I had just woken up. The enthusiasm and confidence that I will publish Awaken Yourself, Book 1 on 11/11/2020 grew with each typed word. 4 days and 77 hours later after a continuous writing session, a 45-page book was ready and seemed to have the potential to alleviate suffering. It was uploaded on Amazon on 11/11/2020 at 11:11 p.m. That's how it all turned out. My soul smiled.

I had a blockage that always kept me from publishing, and I had just managed to remove it. With a renewed energy, I brought Book 1 in harmony with my desire to do good, and books 2, 3, 4, 5, 6 and 7 will melodically complete what I started here.

I put my heart, smile and joy into every word.

Everything you can imagine is real.
Trust your intuition.

Cristina Joy

**Lots of people start things; few are able to finish.
Why? They don't trust themselves to get to the end.**

Will you finish what you started?

PART I : AWAKENING

Chapter 1: Win before you begin

It was 2006, summer. It was one of those days when I completely lost confidence that I could navigate the difficult road ahead. Confused by failure after failure, depressions not shared with anyone, bad choices after bad choices, more and more painful challenges and deeply disappointed by everything that life meant, in general, I walked aimlessly, on the streets of a hot Bucharest.

Sweat dripped from my forehead, straight into my eyes. The clothes had become visibly wet from the profuse sweat, and the "firm" sneakers made in China were carelessly dipping into the hot asphalt, which melted under every step, as if preparing to swallow me completely. It wouldn't have bothered me.

"Even the most beautiful flowers grow from the mud."

I was looking down and going nowhere. The moment I changed my direction again, and the wind seemed to be blowing a little, alleviating the discomfort of very high temperatures, a post-it appeared out of nowhere on my feet with the letters in hand: "look at the sky". My first thought?

- "What idiot dared to write that?"

I was in a state where nothing seemed like a good idea to me, not even to look at the sky. I continued on my way, looking down. Only a few minutes later I noticed again, at my feet, the same post-it with the message "look at the sky". For a second, I frowned and wondered.

- "How the hell did this get here?"

I didn't care too much, anyway. So, I continued to see my way to nowhere, with the same gaze on the asphalt. It wasn't long before the post-it appeared at my feet again. The same annoying and, as it were, insistent message, "look at the sky."

For a second, as if exasperated by the message of that post-it, I stopped and looked at the sky. I immediately looked down, with a flash of anger and answering in my mind:

"I looked at the sky. So what?"

I hadn't finished my mental dialogue, because I realized that I felt a little better as soon as I looked at the sky for a second. With surprise and curiosity, I wondered in my mind if I should look at the sky again, as if it were a vital decision in my life. I finally managed to look up from the asphalt that looked like a soft rubber, in which I sank even deeper, when I was standing still.

I looked at the sky, as if I was looking at it for the first time then. Maybe it was really the first time I'd looked at it. With 100% presence, with amazement, with admiration, with humility for the power it had over me. I realized that, just looking at the sky, I had forgotten for a few moments everything that was running, repeatedly, in my head.

Everything was perfect. The sky was clear, it was warm, it was simple, it was great, it was like a painting, it was freedom, it was escape, it was carefree, it was clear mind, it was clear thought, it was hope. Somehow, the mental cloud that I had carefully carried all the way with me, was now turning into the sun.

I felt the energy flow through my whole body, giving me tingles of happiness. A tear broke out spontaneously and slid down my cheek, as if competing with the drops of sweat that flowed profusely, and a smile fell inexplicably on my face.

"*It'll be fine!*", something in me told me.

I believed it with all my being. Why? I do not know!

When I managed to look away from the sky, I noticed on the bench in front of me a handsome young man, with brown hair and a strange smile on his face. He was dressed in white and had a post-it notes and a pen in his hand. Next to him was a black backpack with an open zipper.

Before I knew it, he asked me:

- *Would you have preferred to put an obstacle in your way and fall, in order to look at the sky faster?*

- *Do you know you've been circling for over an hour?*

Still confused and without the slightest idea if he was right that I had been circling for more than an hour, all I managed to articulate was:

- *Aaaaa, I don't know!*

- *What's bothering you? Do you want to talk?* he asked in a warm tone.

- *I don't want to talk about this.*

- *Stay here for a while!* he told me as he showed me the place next to him.

I was tired from walking so much, so, with my head bowed, I sat down next to him on the bench.

I couldn't articulate other words, and he, the perfect stranger, seemed to understand this and did not insist on questions.

We looked at the sky together for a few minutes, after which, he got up from the bench and said some words that remained imprinted in my memory and in my soul:

Don't finish until you really start.

Real life only begins when you fail and when you learn to overcome failures. Failures are the greatest gifts.

That's the only way to learn and grow.

Look at the sky every time you feel like you can't do it anymore, it helps.

Then continue. Every single time! When you feel you can't, you must!

He took a few steps, as if he were leaving. After a few more steps he stopped, stared into my eyes, and said with a warm smile:

Look at the sky!

I took on his warm smile instantly, and as he lost his way in the distance, I looked up at the sky and smiled, with a regained desire to overcome the challenges I had.

Such guides appear when we least expect it, but most of the time, exactly when we need it most.

"The most awaited guides are those who help us discover the source of our own power."

- Cristina Joy

From time to time, we all need a guide, a word of encouragement, a renewed inner hope that will bring us back to the waterline. Sometimes that guide is a stranger, other times that guide is a quote that gets in your way, maybe an act of kindness that someone does for you, or maybe the guide is an idea from a book that gets into your hands, seemingly by chance.

No matter what form it takes, the guide always has the best intentions for us. Maybe a guide is under these heartfelt words for you.

Allow these lines to touch your heart and guide you to the answer you are looking for.

If a line, an idea, a story, a thought or a word from this book creates in you that "A-ha!" moment, the goal has been achieved.

In life and in everything you do, you will only win if you decide not to give up.

"When you are in a dark place you tend to think you have been buried; What if you were planted?"

The game does not end when you fail. On the contrary, it is only then that it really begins. The game only ends when you decide to stop playing.

I challenge you to continue this game called life until you master the easiest way to win. Keep going and don't stop for nothing until you are full of joy, happiness, vitality, quality relationships, contribution, material things you want, feelings of fulfilment. Yes, you have the right to whatever you want. You can get everything you want.

"The challenge you are in today is developing the strength you need tomorrow."

Don't stop playing until you develop the strength to keep reinventing yourself whenever needed.

Don't stop playing until you have mastered the rules of the game. Don't stop playing until, being the master of the rules, you now know how to break the rules so well and win in a way that no one thinks it is possible to win. Don't stop playing until you come out the winner.

Decide here and now, whatever you have in mind as the ultimate goal, that the game only ends when you win, regardless of duration, time, failures or obstacles.

Failures and obstacles do not stop you from playing, they are just pieces of the game, which must be put aside gracefully, so that you can continue, wiser and stronger, to the next level.

I challenge you to apply this strategy to this book as well.

Win before you start.

Millions of books are sold worldwide.

And, guess what?

Studies show that 85% of them never get read.

Can you imagine millions of people spending money on books and not even getting to read them?

Why is this happening?

"The results you enjoy in your life now are either the result of your focus or the result of your distractions. Distractions are getting you out of the game. The choice is always yours. "

- Cristina Joy

I'll tell you! So many things have been created to hunt, capture and consume our attention that it is difficult to fight them and consciously decide what is really worth our time and attention and what is not.

Our brain is stimulated millions of times with reward chemicals, received by our body with ecstasy and ignorance, from social media data, TV, phones & so on.

We are subtly manipulated and redirected from the world we consider real to the virtual world. A world that does not exist, that is not at all as pleasant as the real one, but which, through technological engineering, has learned to hack our behaviour and make us more and more dependent on it. Our attention is drawn like a magnet by the screens, and every time we try to get our heads out of them, back to reality, the magnet becomes stronger, and our head returns, like a submissive slave, bound in chains, to this screen.

We are, as it were, sedated, asleep, and fed with adiction.

We are far from human connection, far from compassion, far from patience, far from empathy, far from real care, far from emotional support, far from gratitude, far from true friends, far from the real stories of our lives, in a false world, full of filters, stories and images, which constantly beg our acceptance.

I challenge you to decide here and now to recoup your investment in this book, to aim to read it to the end and to do all the proposed exercises and madness, with an open heart, with curiosity and without judging anything as good or bad, true or untrue.

"If you postpone, if you put off later, if you give the power of this present moment on a promise of an imagined future, you leave your life in random hands and the future at the expense of an invisible autopilot, which has no direction, vision or intention as to make your life better, more fun, more fulfilling and more conscious, here and now, in the only moment that really matters. "

- Cristina Joy

My promise:

I, ..., promise to read this book by ...., to be open, curious and to release any desire to judge the content. I promise, here and now, to invest more time to learn HOW to think. I will do the exercises in this book, even if it will mean that I have to think, reflect, explore areas that I have not explored before. My intention for this book is to help me evolve into unconditional happiness and I am willing to do the necessary work for that.

Signed,   Date,
....

I challenge you to develop your critical thinking, not to take anything as it is from what you find in this book, not to take anything as it is from what you find around you, to question everything that is here and everything that you consider now as true.

This is how the awakening begins.

This book came to me with speed, clarity and absolute certainty. It had to get into your hands as soon as possible. Yes, in your hands.

If you read these lines, take a deep breath, put a smile on your face and repeat after me:

"I'm exactly where I need to be, I'm doing exactly what I should be doing."

There are no coincidences. Everything happens for a reason.

You chose to read these lines, out of millions available all over the world and on the internet, because you needed to read this.

This book overflowed from my pain, from the pain I feel inside when I hear all these sad stories from friends of my friends who committed suicide, from the pain I feel knowing that more and more people are depressed, in despair, suffering from anxiety, hopelessness, sadness, frustration, unhappiness...

If you read these lines, it means that you also resonate with my pain and that you are open to receive a way to participate in changing what you do not like around you, by becoming a living example of what you want to see around you.

The road to happiness begins with awareness of the source of unhappiness.

It breaks my heart to hear people who want to give up everything and say: "I can't do anything, I'm too small."

That is what society made each of us believe. That we are "the little and helpless self."

This idea is so far from the truth.

"If you think you're too small to make a difference you haven't spent a night with a mosquito."

Why believe everything you are told?
Why give up life so easily?
Why put your power on the tray so easily?
Why let outside circumstances dictate how you feel inside?

If there are times when you feel like giving up, it's ok. I'm not asking you to deny how you feel.

On the contrary, I want you to embrace and accept all the emotions you feel, because they are valid.

Your emotions are the best indicator and when you feel down, all it means is that you have forgotten who you are.

When you are in a dark place, all you need is to remember who you really are and things will settle down again.

All you need is to constantly remember who you are.

Please consciously choose to read with your heart and not with your mind, the following lines:

"Do not resist your pain.
Surrender to grief, despair, fear, loneliness or whatever form of suffering takes.
Witness it without labelling it mentally.
Allow it to be there.
Embrace it.
Then see how the miracle of surrender transmutes deep suffering into deep peace. "

- **Eckhart Tolle**

It took me a while to accept and understand the truth and depth behind these words.

To honor the pain, to accept it and to hand it over to peace.

Sounds easy, but is it easy?

It takes a lot of awareness and practice.

Even this quote alone has the power to put an end to human suffering and pave the way for happiness, but only if we can take a little time to truly understand the real power behind these simple words. The rush in our lives makes us unconsciously intensify our suffering.

"Until we understand them, we will be slaves to our emotions."

- Cristina Joy

Imagine how, all your life, you reacted to the circumstances around you.

Something happened and you felt certain emotions by default.

No one has explained to you how to get to the point where you can easily observe when you are suffering, so that you can accept the suffering, so that you can detach yourself from it, so that you can consciously let it go and consciously recover your inner peace.

That is about to change.

It's all about becoming really awake and aware of what you can control and what you can't control.

This is the only way you can accept and find peace when you face anything beyond your control.

Sounds like magic, doesn't it?

It's not magic, it's exactly who you really are and one of your super powers is that you can observe your thoughts, emotions and actions and change what you don't like about them, having as an eternal compass, the way you feel at all times.

We grew up pointing the finger when someone or something makes us feel bad. We grew up wanting more of that something that makes us feel good. We grew up believing that feeling good comes from the outside and it is random.

All the suffering you have experienced all your life is not caused by your environment, it is not caused by society, it is not caused by your job, it is not caused by any "morona", it is not caused by anything outside of you.

All the suffering you have experienced all your life, as well as all the happiness you have experienced in your whole life, is caused by your mind, by the thoughts you think about anything and the meaning you give to those thoughts.

Have you ever suffered on the outside? No. Everything is inside and it is given by what you choose to think about each event.

"Well, you know, the mind is nothing.
The mind is only a bunch of thoughts.
Thoughts about the past and the future, that is all a mind is.
But, the heart is a centre of stillness, of quietness, of absolute peace.
When you rest your mind in your heart, you feel a joy and a bliss, that overwhelms you and you will know.
Surrender your mind to your heart and you will feel it. "

- Robert Adams

You are bigger, stronger and more in control of yourself than you think and as you remember who you really are, you will begin to feel this in your body.

You will begin to feel this with every cell in you and you will carry that feeling with you every day for the rest of your life.

"One's mind, once stretched by a new idea, never regains its original dimensions."

-

Oliver Wendell Holmes Sr.

Try this:

1. Remember a time when you suffered enormously.
What were you saying to yourself in those moments? What was the posture of your body? What energy level did you have? What were you constantly thinking about?

_____
_____
_____
_____
_____
_____
_____
_____
_____

2. Remember a time when you were mega happy.
What were you saying to yourself in those moments? What was the posture of your body? What energy level did you have? What were you constantly thinking about?

_____
_____
_____
_____
_____
_____
_____
_____
_____

I welcome you on the journey of awakening.

Chapter 2: Bringing Darkness to Light

How it all started...

I joyfully sleepwalked through my life until I was 29 years old.

I have never wondered why I am here, what is the purpose of my existence and all the other deep questions, but I must admit that I have always been accompanied by the feeling that I am protected, loved and guided.

It's like I've always had my inner voice, which, no matter how hard / bad it was, it always whispered to me.

- *"It's alright. It's going to get better. Keep going."*

My childhood was wonderful and hard, full of contrasting experiences, just like yours, most likely.

What made the difference for me was that in my attempt to get rid of the bad side and the fear that plagued me when people around me became violent or screamed in my environment, I found that I could soften what was happening with a smile and by sitting centered, while I seemed unaffected by all those negative behaviors.

Don't be fooled by this.

Every time I was in a violent scenario, I was terrified. Fear flowed through every cell of my body.

I can't tell you exactly when or how I started using this defense mechanism.

Imagine this: my superpower to stop the violence: a smile and pretending that everything is ok.

I have no idea how I adopted this, but my mind and soul said it was a good idea.

Believe it or not, it worked every time.

My reward? The surrounding conflicts stopped immediately, those who were angry remembered to smile, the violence turned into play.

Somehow, my defense mechanism was working.

Woohoo! I couldn't believe my eyes.

I was breaking patterns before it became popular to do that. Before I even knew what a pattern of behavior was and and that there are techniques to interrupt them.

I was a personal development trainer as a child, with a technique invented and permanently implemented by me.

That's how I saved this smile of mine as a "default" mode and to this day, you can rarely find a time when you can see me without it, even if more than 30 years have passed since I started using it, unconsciously, to protect my well-being and that of those around me.

"If you want your children to be intelligent, read them fairy tales. If you want them to be more intelligent, read them more fairy tales."

-Albert Einstein

What Einstein pointed out here is that our intelligence, as children, develops when we have the opportunity to expand our imagination, to be free, to dream, to be exposed to new ideas.

Our challenge is that we were exposed to reality and the state education system, where our imagination was beaten to the core, with tons of texts that we had to memorize if we wanted to pass the class. This is how our intelligence and creativity faded, year after year, as our "smartness" increased or, better said, as our ability to become parrots who can memorize information increased.

As I grew up, I took as my truth everything I was told as a child.

The good part, the bad part, the beautiful part, the ugly part, the shameful part.

So it is that I grew up having as absolute truths all the things that those around me believed and I tacitly and unconsciously accepted them as mine, without any doubt.

That's how I woke up as an adult, pulling an imaginary, huge bag with everything the environment made me think I was.

What was I carrying after me?

What hung the hardest. Shame about the negative events in my life, the fear that I will never have enough, the fear that I am not good enough, the guilt for the mistakes I made, the inability to change the past, the expectations of others, the expectations of society and my family.

Pretty hard stuff, so one day, when I got tired of being who I was told to be, I decided to let go of the bag with shame, fear, mistakes, let go of the imaginary helplessness and expectations of others and create my own expectations of me.

I put aside all the mental limitations that those around me planted in my head and I left, without apology, after everything they told me that I can't be, I can't do and I can't have.

It wasn't about them anymore. From that moment on, everything had become something personal, between me and me.

I became restless, in constant search of that something, that something that I didn't even know what it was. So I learned more and more, I worked harder and harder, I traveled more and more, I experienced more and more, I got more and more things.

I exceeded the limits of what a little girl from a modest town in Romania was supposed to be, do and have.

Everything was as if I became a Duracell battery that was turned ON and the only way I was operating was to do, to do, to do, to do, to do and to do, without stopping.

Let me show myself that I can!

Duracell was, in fact, one of my nicknames.

I told myself: "That's probably how happiness looks like!"

As long as I always planned and did, planned and did, got and became, got and became even more, everything was ok, because there was never time to stop and reflect:

"What am I doing all this for?"

There was no space for what I considered, at the time, to be "stupid questions". I did what I knew best. I immersed myself in even more hours of work.

That's how I ended up, in my adult life, working +16 hours a day, sleeping between 1-4 hours a night and if you had asked me how I'm doing, I would have answered that everything is going great.

Mhm.

Great, until one day when my whole universe collapsed.

At that very moment in time, when I experienced a massive mental breakdown, I really stopped and started questioning everything.

My awakening began with unbearable suffering.

I was done. Finished. Destroyed.

I was exhausted.

Duracell had run out of resources.

After working for over 16 hours a day, for months, without proper rest, my mind, body and soul were exhausted, out of their natural state and completely out of alignment.

I didn't even know the word "alignment" in the context of mind, body, soul. Everything was the same in my mind.

So, totally unplanned, I really found out its meaning when I experienced the lack of alignment of the three.

What started happening to me shocked me.

I was thinking something in my thinking process, but I was saying something completely different and doing something completely different then what I was thinking and saying. I had lost control over myself and that was the most shocking part of my life.

Can you imagine thinking about saying something, saying something different and then doing something completely different with 0 control over what you think, say and do?

Oh my God!

I still get goosebumps when I remember how I felt in those moments.

It was as if we were three different people in the same body, only that the three people did not talk to each other and had a "mind" of their own.

One was thinking something, the other was saying something completely different, and the third one was doing something completely opposite. As if their goal was to defy each other.

Me, in this whole equation? Just a helpless spectator.

In other words, I felt like I was torn to three different pieces and I couldn't get back together.

I was so scared, especially because I had no idea what was going on.

It was like I had my own madhouse inside me.

I couldn't think, say or do anything in alignment.

Simultaneously, like a cherry on top, I had just ended a toxic relationship, where gaslighting (manipulating someone, through psychological means, to doubt one's own mental health) was the order of the day.

I was constantly criticized, I was asked daily to change in different ways, I was insulted, I was manipulated to believe that I had not heard things I had heard, I was manipulated to believe all sorts of bad things about myself.

"Someone I once loved gave me a box full of darkness.
It took me years to understand that this, too, was a gift."

- Mary Oliver

I could not see the blessings disguised under all these experiences at that time.

Oh my God!

I was in such a dark place and my confusion exploded.

Everything collapsed in a huge STOP.

I couldn't go on with anything, not even for a day.

The first day I stopped, I felt lost.

What added even more to my pain was that people around me could not notice anything. I looked "normal" on the outside. Obvious! All the clutter was inside.

In those moments I couldn't focus on anything good, because I couldn't see anything good. All I could see was a huge dark cloud and a lot of fog, full of everything that had happened to me. I could not see a way out of my condition.

It was as if I were present, but absent.

It was like I was on Earth, but I wasn't.

It was as if everything felt real, but it wasn't.

I was in a confused, very confused state.

I gathered all the feelings in a valley of sadness, frustration, mourning, brain fog, lack of self-control, lack of self-confidence, doubt, emptiness, anger, fear, insecurity, inadequacy, the feeling of "out of place", "obsolete" and I could not see any solution.

I felt, for the first time, that all my life I had gone with full speed forward to nowhere.

That's exactly what I did.

From the outside, I seemed that I had everything figured out. I seemed to know what I wanted to do with my life, I was great at finding opportunities in anything, embracing change with every step and keeping myself busy all the time.

But on the inside, oh my God!

That was a different story.

It was time to bring the darkness to the surface.

Only after experiencing this burnout, this exhaustion, this total surrender, did I truly realize that I was always busy to run away from the feeling of emptiness, past traumas and insecurity.

What I had never realized before was that inside I was carrying a wounded inner child.

My wounded inner child was always there, in the shadows, waiting for me to stop and give her a chance to heal.

On the other hand, I was always on the run, busy, working incessantly, to avoid this stop, this confrontation and this healing, unconsciously.

Even if, after over 10 years of working at maximum levels, without a well-defined goal, I was finally able to articulate my goal: to become a top global trainer, to educate, uplift and teach the science of well-being to millions of people of souls and to stop the global suffering, I was still repeating the same patterns over and over again.

I had not brought to light the darkness of my childhood.

I had this great goal hidden somewhere in my heart, but in the foreground of my mind was the same message, as if it was written in bold:

"Keep doing, doing and doing. Don't stop for nothing! "

I continued like this, like a hamster on a wheel, scared that the world would stop, if I stopped running.

Yes, that little hamster wanted to save humanity from suffering, while suffocating in deep suffering.

It was clear that I had to save myself first, so I stopped.

After over 10 years of running continuously in my hamster wheel, I managed to stop.

This stop was what my mind, body, and soul wanted from me.

I felt so disconnected from everyone, but most of all, I felt completely disconnected from myself.

Somehow, even in those moments, I managed to hear the voice that always assured me that everything would be fine.

I was in a boat, in the middle of nature, in the Danube Delta, surrounded by water, which always calmed my soul.

Vivid green, deep silence, warm breeze, all felt with every cell of my confused tanned cheek. In the background, from time to time, the sound of the water hitting the boat, reminded me of being in the here and now, in the only place that really matters. I watched in amazement the beauty of everything around me and managed to get out, for a few moments, of the drama movie that was running on repeat in my head.

I hear and feel the voice, as if happening again now:

"- You will be fine. You know this."

From the bottom of the abyss, that was all I needed to hear, to start creating a way out.

It was as if until then I had my head stuck in a huge cloud, from where I could not see anything, and when I heard those words that cloud dissolved, like a balloon disappearing from the landscape, after stabbing it with a needle.

Something in me seemed to click at that moment and I started working on rebuilding, in me, the confidence that I know what I have to do.

I put my recovery in the hands of the same person who put me in this situation, in the first instance: me.

I promised myself that I would gather and glue all the detached pieces of myself back and that I would rebuild myself from scratch.

The first stage of my recovery was sleep, a lot of sleep.

I was suffering from chronic lack of sleep and in the first days of recovery I felt that I was constantly slipping into a black hole, from which I can no longer get out.

I have few to no memories from the early days. All I remember clearly is that the first day of sleeping without an alarm, the first day without pushing myself to do things, translated into 16 hours of deep sleep.

"The dark night of the soul is a journey into light, a journey from your darkness into the strength and hidden resources of your soul."

- Caroline Moss

After a few days of adequate sleep, the light began to find its way to me.

Tears come to my eyes now as I type, as I remember the moment I woke up rested, after so many years of continuous exhaustion, and said to myself:

"It's ok, you'll be ok!" while out of my body, the anxiety and feeling that I should do something, instead of resting, began to disappear.

This was the first natural impulse of self-love, which I had never experienced before, in my whole existence, being busy pushing myself to do more, to be more and to have more.

This was the first time in my life that I just allowed myself to be. Without doing anything for a while.

I remembered that I was a human being.

And that the purpose of a human being is to BE, not to DO.

From that moment on, an expansive journey unfolded before my eyes.

Since then, I have not stopped growing as a being WHO IS, and now I am ready to lead you on the path of least resistance, as a guide that helps you remember your way back home, from an unknown mountain.

So, if you have been through your own darkness or maybe you still are, take me by the hand, as we are about to embark on a journey of remembrance. Your journey back home, to peace, to love, to unconditional happiness.

"You can truly appreciate light only after you have known darkness."

- **Cristina Joy**

Try this:

1. Remember a moment in your life when I felt defeated, disoriented, lost. Where were you? With whom? What had happened? How did you feel?

_____

_____

_____

_____

_____

_____

_____

_____

_____

2. Be aware of how you have grown since then. How did you evolve after the darkness came to light?

What lessons did you take? How did you become stronger? How did you reinvent yourself as a result of that moment in your life?

_____

_____

_____

_____

_____

_____

_____

_____

_____

3. What other negative experiences / feelings do you feel you need to bring to light? Be honest with yourself. What are you running from?

_____
_____
_____
_____
_____
_____
_____
_____
_____
_____

4. Why is it important to bring darkness to light? How are this experiences/ feelings affecting your life?

_____
_____
_____
_____
_____
_____
_____
_____
_____
_____

Chapter 3: Reset time. The Story of the Zen Master

" Zen is a kind of unlearning. It teaches you how to drop that which you have learned, how to become unskillful again, how to become a child again, how to start existing without mind again, how to be here without any mind."

- Rajneesh

Once upon a time there was a Zen Master. This Zen Master had all the happiness, peace and wisdom in the world that everyone aspires to.

In his community, there was a very wealthy man, with a very important function, who had palaces, riches and absolutely everything a man could want.

He lacked only one thing: happiness.

He always felt nervous, agitated, frustrated, unhappy.

Although he had everything he ever wanted and was envied by everyone around him, he felt miserable.

The Zen master, on the other hand, although he had a very modest house, modest clothes, modest resources, seemed to have exactly what this very wealthy man lacked: happiness.

Every time you saw this Zen Master in the courtyard, you could easily read on his face serenity, peace, and happiness in its purest form.

The Zen Master had been in high demand all his life.

Many people wanted to learn his magic and discover the secrets of his happiness and wisdom.

For years, the Zen Master had shared his wisdom with all who came to his gate.

It's just that Master Zen was now old and wanted to use his energy for gardening and the things that brought him joy. The Zen Master wanted total peace from now on, and he no longer accepted students.

One day, when the unhappiness of the wealthy man had reached its peak, he decided to go to the Zen Master and ask him to teach him the secrets of happiness.

Arriving at the gate of the Zen Master, he began to shout desperately:

- *Zen Master! Zen Master! Zen Master!*

The Zen Master, who was serenely watering his flowers in the garden, put down the sprinkler and calmly approached this unknown man at his gate.

Then this wealthy man, in an aggressive and arrogant tone, said to the Zen Master:

- *Zen Master, you must teach me how to be zen! I'm very unhappy!*

The Zen Master smiled and said to the wealthy man:

- *Let's discuss this matter over a cup of tea.*

The Zen Master opened the gate and invited this wealthy man to his modest house for a cup of tea.

When the tea was ready to be served, the Zen Master began pouring the tea into his guest's cup.

He continued to pour into the cup until the cup was full. The Zen Master did not stop. He continued to pour until the cup began to pour out.

At first, the wealthy man said nothing, but seeing that the Zen Master continued to pour tea into the full cup, and the tea was scattering everywhere, he jumped out of his chair and decided to use his aggressive and arrogant tone again, snarling at the Zen Master:

- *Zen Master, what the hell are you doing? Stop it! Don't you see that the cup is full and the tea is scattered everywhere?*

Hearing this, the Zen Master, who was still pouring tea into the full cup, smiled, looked at him, stopped pouring tea into the overflowing cup, and then said to the wealthy man:

- *Yes, the cup is full. Just like your mind! Where do you want to put new information?*

The lesson here is that sometimes we have the feeling that we have to learn more things, when in reality we have to unlearn many things.

We are born with an empty cup.

And in this cup, from the first years of life, our family puts information, society puts information, the education system puts information, our teachers put information, our colleagues put information, our friends put information, until one day when, our cup becomes full and when we want to add new information, which resonates with us, we have no room to put it.

How much of the information in your cup is who you really are?

Maybe you were told that you are not good enough, that you are ugly, that you are stupid, that you are too short, that you are too tall, that you do not deserve anything, that you are bad.

Imagine that everything you were told was stored in your cup.

But, is this information stored who you really are or is it just information gathered in your cup, from the environment, when you were not aware and did not have the power to filter it?

And now comes the question.

Do you think that you have to learn more or that you have to unlearn certain things in order to make room for new information that will change your life?

"In some sense our ability to open the future will depend not on how well we learn anymore but on how well we are able to unlearn."

- Alan Kay

 Try this:

Travel back in time and remember some negative words that were said to you when you were younger, that affected you and that, perhaps, still affect your life today.

The words that were said to me and that affected me/ still affect me are:

_____
_____
_____
_____
_____
_____
_____
_____
_____
_____
_____
_____
_____
_____

Are these words true? (Circle)
Yes.   No.

The positive words I consciously choose to replace the negative words I was told as a child are:

_____
_____
_____
_____
_____
_____
_____
_____
_____
_____
_____
_____

Are these words true? (Circle)
　Yes.　　　No.

The most beautiful part?

You have the power to decide now what is true and what is not.

"The most useful piece of learning for the uses of life is to unlearn what is untrue."

— Antisthenes

CHALLENGE:

Write messages of encouragement on your post-it notes or often put alarms on your phone with positive messages that you would like to hear from those around you.

Example:

I'm good enough. You're good enough.
I am an extraordinary man/ woman. You are an extraordinary man.
I deserve the best. You deserve the best.
I accept myself as I am. I accept you as you are.
I love myself as I am. I love you the way you are.
I am a wonderful human being. You are a wonderful human being.
I am worthy. You are worthy.

"Until you learn to appreciate yourself, those around you will not appreciate you either. Until you learn to respect yourself, those around you will not respect you either. Until you learn to love yourself, those around you will not love you either. At least, not as you deserve to be truly appreciated, respected and loved.
It all starts with you. "

- Cristina Joy

PART 2: ACCEPTANCE

Chapter 4: Who are you?

Awareness is not about who you are, but rather about who you are not.

Write in a few words who you are:

_____

_____

_____

_____

_____

_____

_____

_____

And now, if everything you've written is your first name, last name, qualifications, jobs, skills, or anything else society has told you you are, I want you to write who you are again.

Who do you think you are, not who society and the environment told you you are:

_____

_____

_____

_____

_____

_____

_____

_____

Awakening to happiness is related to the expansion of your consciousness and the beginning of a journey with small and sure steps towards understanding your own existence on this planet.

Awakening is related to this game called life.

There's so much noise about finding yourself.

Finding yourself is not exactly how this whole thing works. You are not a 10 pounds note lost in the pocket of last winter's clothes.

You are not lost, though, sometimes you may feel that you are.

Your true self is exactly where you are, buried under cultural conditioning, blocked by other people's opinions and suffocated by the inaccurate conclusions you drew as a child and as an adult about who you are.

Awakening to happiness and finding the self is actually a return to self, an unlearning, a deeper digging, a reminder of who you were before people laid their hands on you. Then a deep acceptance of one's own truth.

I invite you to travel back in time and imagine the first day you came into this world.

Close your eyes for a second and visualize your arrival in this reality. There is no right or wrong way to do this. You probably won't remember all the details or maybe you won't remember anything. That's ok. Just imagine how your arrival here happened.

After nine months in your mother's womb, you decided to get to know the outside world. You were a miracle. You were such an adorable baby, even when you were crying.

Your mother received you as well as she knew, and you felt safe from the first moments when she held you to her chest, because you easily remembered her warmth, her energy and her familiar voice, ever since you grew up comfortably in her belly. You came here as pure positive energy. You knew how to experience joy for no reason. Happiness was natural to you. Your main focus was to explore the world around you.

You had no beliefs about who you were, no negative thoughts about yourself, about life, about your family, about society, about the world.

You didn't care what people thought of you, you were too busy exploring the environment and you enjoyed this experience called life.

You did not judge anyone and you were happy to live in the present moment.

Just remember the first giggles you generously shared with the world around you for no reason, just because that's how you were, happiness in its purest form. You were born happiness in pure form.

You weren't afraid of anything.

Just remember your mother's despair when you threw yourself in front of cars with a smile on your face, when you enthusiastically put your little hands in the oven or when you were speeding towards dangerous animals. You had no idea that those around you were preparing to teach you fear.

You didn't need reasons to smile. You just smiled and did what you felt. You filled people's souls with joy, effortlessly. You had no idea that those around you were preparing to teach you when to be happy and when not.

Although there were many worries, problems, shortcomings and daily challenges around you, you sailed gracefully past them, you kept playing and sharing joy, like a master in enjoying souls, that you were.

Just think of a baby in your life now.

Does this baby have such power over you?

Does your soul rejoice in the presence of a child? Can you be serious when a baby or a child smiles at you?

How does the presence of a child make you feel?

Whenever you have the opportunity, for the joy of refreshing your understanding, observe the children, in the park, at home, observe them in their natural state, so that you can delight your soul in the memory of how it feels to be really awake and happy.

Joy, love, play, curiosity, serenity, presence.

" Children are happy because they don't have a file in their minds called " All the things that could go wrong" "

- Marianne Williamson

You, the adult? Do you have that file or are you happy?

 Try this:

Write here all the scenarios that keep you in place, that stop you from living your dreams. What are the scenarios you create in your head? Are they real? What evidence do you have that they are real?

_____

_____

_____

_____

_____

_____

Chapter 5: Who Decides Who You Are?

You were very awake and happy as a baby.

As life went on, and you grew up, you took on board a lot of social and cultural conditioning.

So what went wrong?

You have successfully learned how to deal with the outside world, but no one has explained to you how the inner world works, how your body works and maybe, most importantly, how your mind works.

You see, your mind collects absolutely everything that comes in contact with your five senses (sight, hearing, smell, taste and touch).

The most important part is that most of the impressions collected in this way are "saved" unconsciously, and you have no power to consciously sort out what enters and what does not enter there, in your subconscious mind. Every sound, every smell, every taste, every touch, every sight you have gathered, everything is saved in your mind.

Whatever comes your way is saved there. You can't stop anything.

Some of this information you are able to extract and use, most of it you are not able to extract and use, but it is there, working in the background.

All this creates a constant impact, in different ways, in your life. So, it is important to remember that absolutely all the information from when you are awake or sleeping is automatically saved in your mind from your first day on this Earth and you have no control over it.

Anything that comes your way will plant things in your head and leave. You can't stop this. TV, society, social media, movies, radio, friends, family, teachers, bosses, strangers.

Even if you say, "I don't like this person," you still can't stop this automatic process.

Prepare your armor, as if you were preparing to face an unpleasant truth. When you have it ready, keep reading.

I will tell you in a very harsh and direct way, that your mind is the rubbish bin of society. Relax! Mine is, too.

It sounds a little extreme, I know, but it's very true. The mind accumulates, accumulates, accumulates and accumulates. It doesn't sort anything, it just accumulates.

You can take this trash, regardless of its contents, and you can make a wonderful fertilizer out of it or you can live in this rubbish, navigating hard through the dirt, only that the latter choice leads to suffering.

That's the choice you have. What do you get in your mind? You can't control. What can you control? What do you choose to use and what do you choose not to use from everything that "enters".

The sad part? Over 90% of the world's population does not control even this part, because they are not awakened to the understanding that they have this power.

Therefore, it is becoming easier to notice more and more people with compulsive behavior.

I noticed this just this morning.

I went shopping at a grocery store in central London. Normally, the store opened at 6:30 am. It was 6:28 am when I sat quietly in line.

We waited for two minutes, and from now on we were all waiting for the doors to open.

It's 6:32, and the people in the queue get agitated because the store doesn't open on time.

Me? In my zen mode, I just thought they were humans, not robots, and maybe they were late. It happened before.

Because of "morona" and because there were fewer people on the streets, therefore fewer customers per hour

so early in the morning, many businesses in the area decided to change their opening hours.

The only thing? Me and the other few people waiting in front of the store had no idea that this store decided the same thing.

Seeing that there was no intention in opening the store, very calm, I approached to read the program on the window. The was an announcement that, from now on, the store will open at 7 am.

To help the other people waiting in line, I explained that the store will open at 7 am. Do you think anyone thanked me for informing them?

No way. They started knocking on the window, to the employees in the store, to tell them to open, that it's 6:30 am.

The employees of the store told them that the store opens, from now on, at 7 am, and most of those who were waiting, started screaming, talking badly to the employees and, finally, leaving very irritated. Let's be honest.

Was the response of these people conscious or compulsive?

I don't want to point out anything right / wrong, but truth be told, all this global noise and all the negative mess spread through out all communication channels translated into even more compulsive behavior.

Make an honest assessment.

On a scale from 1-10 how compulsive are you and also from 1-10 how much are you really conscious in your life? Circle the number that you think fits your current situation.

Compulsive:

1–2–3–4–5–6–7–8–9–10

Conscious:

1–2–3–4–5–6–7–8–9–10

It is important to have a moment of reflection and to be honest with yourself.

Observe yourself carefully and answer the following two questions:

How much of what I do happens consciously?

_____%

How much of what I do happens compulsively? (on autopilot)

_____%

If you study objectively, you will notice that a large part of you happens compulsively.

When you're compulsive, you don't behave the way you want to behave, do you?

You lose your temper, you say a harsh word, you are not polite, you criticize more, you complain about everything, you get angry, you accuse without reason, etc.

There is only one challenge with our lives: life does not happen the way we think it should.

This is the only challenge that we humans have in reality.

Life does not happen as you think it should. That the world and life do not happen the way you want, let's say there is something you can get over.

The challenge is that you don't behave the way you want to.

No one around you behaves exactly the way you want, but if there is only one person who needs to behave the way you want, that person is you. Right?

For things to change and for things to happen the way you want them to happen, you have to craft some inner things.

Do you remember how hard it was to change the direction of travel to a car without power steering?

Do you recognize how easy it is now to change the direction of travel to a car with power steering?

What happened between the two?

A little interior craftsmanship, under the hood, made by an engineer.

That's exactly what you need, in order to be better, a little inner craftsmanship.

So, what you gather over a lifetime doesn't matter so much.

Your ability to use only what you want, from everything you've gathered is the challenge, isn't it?

Can you imagine, for a second, how much mess you have accumulated in your head, from the world, from the news, from society, from social media, from the people around you?

Imagine your mind, on a piece of floating wood, in the middle of a huge sea, green with dirt and pollution.

Now that you are aware of this, you can learn to navigate all the mess.

The suffering you experience in your life comes from the accumulated misery and the inability to sort it out and navigate through it consciously.

When you suffer, you are not really conscious.

Suffering is created in your mind, by the thoughts you think about an event, a situation, a person. Yes?

Then why would you consciously create suffering for yourself?

Did you think a little? Wonderful!

How to clean through all the accumulated dirt?

Bring it to the surface and make it conscious.

Recognize it, accept it and decide that you will not let it influence you.

Only then will you have the freedom to sort out what you want and what you don't want.

Only then will you take the power to decide who you are.

When you become aware of all the misery accumulated throughout your life, I have every confidence that you will do the necessary work to become a truly happy person.

And now that you have that understanding, let's go back to what happened when you grew up.

"Be yourself!" - they told you, while they started to show you that you have to look like this, you have to dress like this, you have to speak in a certain way, you have to sit still in a bench and listen, whether you like it or not, you don't have to ask questions, you have to learn like a little robot and reproduce information, you have to get good grades and people around you will laugh at you if you fail to do so.

How could you grow and become authentic and extraordinary, when you were constantly told what to do, what to think, how to dress and how to behave?

Your joy and ability to be playful have been forcibly transformed into compliance and obedience by others without too many questions.

Your unconditional love for everything around you was suddenly transformed into conditioned love.

As the environment changed, you soon found yourself at school, in constant competition with the children who used to be your playmates, in front of the block.

Cooperation with classmates was deeply discouraged. You grew up, and instead of that pure joy you used to display, you began to harbor in yourself the emotions that life experience has given you: frustration, anger, anxiety, shame, boredom, guilt, and other nuances of negative emotions.

If, in addition to all this, you experienced other traumas in childhood, instead of living in the present moment, you began to live in your head, reliving scenarios, making scenarios, worrying about different scenarios.

Just imagine that you took a small grade and your parents were very strict. Be honest, were you still living in the moment at school, after you took the grade or did you imagine in your head what would happen next at home, when you would present the notebook?

Unconsciously, you exchanged the present moment for past regrets and worries about the future.

The energy you put so easily into the present, into the here and now, has been transformed into time to think. You have unconsciously built an imaginary prison in your mind.

You began to worry, you began to doubt yourself, you began to feel fear, you began to feel unworthy of unconditional love, especially when you were making mistakes.

Only through examples will you better understand what I mean, so I will be honest and vulnerable with you.

Be gentle with me, because it's not easy for me to share my personal stories, especially because I had no plans to share them (although I have hundreds, even thousands). I didn't even imagine that I would remember these specific events from my childhood, they came to my mind with incredible details, now, while I was typing.

Here is another confirmation that everything is saved on the "hard disk", in our subconscious mind.

It was 1993... wow!

Looks like it all happened a lifetime ago.

It's been so long, it's hard to believe, even for me, that I remember so vividly, as if it happened yesterday, how I gathered my beliefs about unworthiness, money, fear, debt, shame, guilt and embarrassment.

I was 7 years old and I had just started Primary School. The school I was enrolled in seemed huge to me, it was colored in green, it took me 5 minutes to walk there and I was just starting to get used to the heavy backpack , the uniform in white and blue, the rigid rules - you shouldn't hear the fly for the 50 minutes of each hour - and the demands that aggressively told me it was time to say goodbye to my childhood play and to the freedom to do what I want.

Only a few days after school began, an elderly lady with white hair, a light-colored cape and white hospital slippers began selling donuts in the school hallway during breaks. She had them in a plastic basin, covered with a white cloth and always had disposable napkins in sight.

At that time, I didn't have any personal money for food, with me, at school. My mother always prepared some food to bring with me.

A large part of my colleagues, on the other hand, bought her donuts every day. I was just drooling every time I saw them eating them happily, with a lot of appetite, in front of me.

One day, the lady with the donuts asked me if I wanted a donut.

I told her I would love one.

She asked me if I had any money.

I told her I had no money.

She told me, "It's okay, take a donut, you'll bring me the money next time."

I replied, "I don't receive any pocket money."

She insisted and gave me the donut.

As a child, I didn't quite understand why she gave me the donut, especially since I had explained to her that I was not getting any pocket money. But I was happy. I said "Thank you" and I devoured the donut I had just received.

The next day, she was in the hallway again and offered me another donut.

This time she didn't ask me anything about money, she offered me the donut, she smiled at me, she told me about her nieces, who love the donuts she makes. I told her about my grandmother, I thanked her and went to eat the donut in class.

The lady with the donuts was looking very similar to my grandmother, who always made me donuts, when I went to the countryside, to visit her. In my mind, I saw her as a dear grandmother, who offered me donuts, so I received the second donut with joy and gratitude.

I felt lucky and blessed to be able to enjoy the donuts I liked so much.

The next day, she offered me another donut.

I must admit that her donuts were fluffy and tasty, and as a child who loved donuts (and still loves them), I said yes and thank you again.

What child would say no to a donut?

I certainly don't.

I felt so happy to serve a donut whenever she came, as if the donuts alleviated a bit of the teacher's rigid tone, the boredom during class and the concept of listening in front of the everyone, quite harshly, during class.

In a short time, my donut paradise turned into hell.

After donut number four, the lady with the donuts changed radically. She stopped smiling and being cute, suddenly.

The break came and as soon as she saw me in the hallway that day, she started pointing her finger at me and started shouting (making sure everyone in school could hear) that I had to pay for the donuts I ate.

I remember perfectly the feeling of shame combined with confusion and misunderstanding of what I had done wrong. I didn't understand what triggered that behavior and why she didn't tell me, personally, if she wanted me to give her money for the donuts she offered me.

I couldn't understand how that good, kind lady turned into such a scary character.

I still remember the fear and shame I felt when she did this scene in front of my colleagues and my sports teacher.

I remember so vividly the expression on her face as she pointed at me, as if I were the biggest trouble maker alive.

She made sure I knew what was waiting for me if I didn't bring her the money.

At the age of 7, after this scene, I was absolutely horrified to go back to school the next day.

Imagine this, I was only 7 years old and I was already in debt.

It doesn't sound like the best start, for a bright future, does it?

After school, I ran home and told my mother all the nonsense. The next day, my mother came to school with me, paid my debt and explained what to do next, in such situations.

After that day, my parents gave me pocket money every day so I could buy what other children were buying.

This situation scared me so much that, from that day on, I never got close to that lady again.

Every time I saw her, I relived the shame I felt the day she pointed her finger at me in front of my classmates and my sports teacher.

Goodbye, pure joy!

I had just successfully installed shame and guilt and I was ready to take them with me.

This was accompanied by uncertainty about how to use the money, self-doubt and self-criticism, because I did not know how to approach this situation better and all this haunted me all my life, from somewhere, in the shadows.

Looking back on my life so far, this small incident has had such a big impact, unconsciously altering the way I started to think, feel and behave around money.

Another thing that happened to me as a child, which may seem small, had a significant impact on me.

It all happened more than 25 years ago, when personal hygiene, self-care information and all the brands that best assured you were not available at a click away, as they are today.

Self-care education was non-existent, so I was given to learn the hard way. Better said, the emotionally painful way.

It was that wonderful time in my life when I started sweating and smelling.

The smell of sweat is probably not like Chanel.

Looking back, I remember as it was yesterday, the confusion I felt.

I didn't understand what was happening to my body, why my hair was growing under my armpit and why I was starting to smell.

Moreover, I was ashamed to ask and I had no idea how to stop all this change.

I washed every morning and every night, but that didn't seem to change the whole process.

I remember struggling to keep my arms very close to my body, hoping that the smell of sweat would not become obvious.

Who does this?

It's hilarious, isn't it?

I laugh out loud now that I remember. I see myself in the classroom where I studied for 8 years, in the second bench in the middle, in my place on the right, in my favorite striped blouse, breathing in the clean smell of cigarettes, which our teacher, in class, emanated every time she passed through the benches and I saw myself holding my arms close to my body, like a soldier, defending himself at the cost of his life, from that which was hidden under his arms.

In the end, I had the courage to ask my parents, and they confirmed to me that it is normal to smell and that I have to wash every day. So I continued to do what I normally did.

Obviously, it wasn't enough just to wash.

During sports classes, my smell of sweat became stronger and more enchanting... not!

One day, as many of us were in this "wonderful" situation and the smell in the gym had become unbreathable, the teacher told us to raise our hand if we smelled bad.

Before I processed her request and denounced myself, like the little scoundrel I was, I was shocked to notice that my dear bank colleague was already pointing at me.

I felt so bad and I was so ashamed that I would have preferred to hide somewhere under the floor of the gym, where no one could see me and not appear back.

We, the smelly ones, were brought out in the spotlight.

We were not given any explanation about the natural changes in the body and how to maintain hygiene, we were not presented with any solution. All the sports teacher told us was that we had to wash ourselves, as if we were unwashed.

The idea was that we washed, only that this did not solve the problem permanently. It was only temporarily.

One of my classmates told me that it doesn't help if you just wash, that you also have to use deodorant.

My light bulb went on instantly. I left home with tears in my eyes, rocking my backpack from one side to another, in sadness, and when I got home, I asked my father for deodorant money.

I didn't tell anyone what happened at school, I kept the shame in me, so my father didn't understand why, suddenly, I asked him for deodorant money or where the idea came from. No matter how hard I tried, I was not able to articulate the shame I lived at school. I just told him that if he didn't give me deodorant money every time I asked for it, I wouldn't go to school.

Without asking too many questions, he complied, gave me money to buy my first deodorant and, look, I joined the league of those who smelled good at school, having a deep compassion for colleagues who could not afford to buy and use deodorant every day.

I knew exactly how they felt.

Anyway, this whole event has instilled in me a deep sense of unworthiness.

What I felt from that moment onward was like an invisible barrier, which conveyed the message that I have to meet certain conditions, to be accepted and that as I am, it is not ok.

I felt that I was not good enough if I did not meet the conditions that those around me were waiting to fulfill.

Not what you have been told or what has happened to you deeply affects you, the huge impact is the way things have been told to you and how it has happened to you, that leaves deep scars in our minds and hearts in the long run.

Have you ever noticed how easy it is for you to remember moments with a strong emotional impact?

They easily stand out in your mind.

The stronger the emotional impact, the more you remember and the more they affect your life, from the bottom of your mind, in a positive or negative way.

After these experiences, what do you think happened to my joy and enthusiasm to go to school, to learn new things?

They evaporated.

I felt judged, I felt insecure, I felt ashamed, I always wondered if I smelled good enough, if the deodorant was good enough, I wondered if I would end up being pointed at again, for the way I smell.

On the outside, I was the same smiling and active child, but on the inside, something had definitely changed.

I began to feel that I did not deserve the support of colleagues and teachers, as I was not sure that I smelled as good as other children, so every day I had this hidden fear that if I did not smell well enough at any time, I could be taken out in front of the class and pointed.

A lot of things happened to me as I grew up, and I will tell them all, one day, because I know that there will be people who will find themselves resonating with them and will be comforted by the thought that embarrassing things did not be happened only to them.

Until then, the memories of the two experiences flowed through my fingers, on the keyboard, as proof that they remained somewhere, stored quite well, in my subconscious mind, as a result of the strong emotional load, from those moments.

These memories hung heavy on my heart, because I was just a child, with a vague idea of life and too little self-understanding. The opinions of those around me were everything to me, and my opinion of me was somewhere, dissipated, against the background of my conscience.

We all have tons of little stories like this, even if we remember them or not, and the accumulation of these little events transformed us from pure energy, which we were, in being conditioned by the environment, family, school, colleagues, experiences with negative emotions, doubts and beliefs.

Somewhere along the way in your life, you were conditioned to feel unworthy, to feel ashamed, to feel guilty, to feel fear, to feel inadequate, to feel that you are more unimportant than others, and you were helped to feel that way, by people around you, who have been conditioned, too.

It is important to take a break for a minute now, to close your eyes and travel back in time, to the days when you were just a child and to remember situations that hang heavy on your heart, situations in which you began to doubt yourself, situations in which you felt ashamed, situations in which you were conditioned to be afraid.

"You are good enough and you are complete. Right now. No proof is required."

- Christie Inge

 Try this:

1. Remember and write down childhood situations when you felt strong negative emotions. Bring the darkness to light, it's time to accept them as part of your life experience.

I'll start.

Ex 1: In the example with donuts. I felt ashamed and guilty. I felt insecure about how to use the money, I felt the fear of debt, I felt that money or its absence are bad things. Money gave me self-doubt and self-criticism, because I did not know how to approach that situation better.

Ex 2: In the example with the smell. I felt unworthy, I felt that I was not good enough, I felt that I do not matter as a human being if I do not meet certain conditions, I felt that I must be ashamed when I do not meet certain conditions, I felt that either I am / I do what others want or I will be pointed out.

Your turn. Describe strong negative events and emotions experienced in childhood:

_____

_____

_____

_____

_____

_____

_____

_____

2. Think now about how these negative events and emotions, from childhood, influence your adult life.

Ex 1: In the example with donuts. In my adult life I gave money a negative connotation. I adopted a mentality of "I never have enough, money is not enough, money gets me in trouble, I better not have money." These internal money conflicts have brought me many problems in my adult life. I didn't know how to manage them, I didn't know how to save them, how to use them wisely, how to avoid financial problems or how to get out of them. Until I got to the root of the problem, I went like shells when it came to money. Only then was I able to guide myself to financial education and transform the relationship I had with money.

Ex 2: In the example with the smell. All that experience made me carry with me the feeling that I am not good enough, it made me care too much about the opinion of others about me, it made me seek the approval of those around me for who I am and what I do. Only when I went to the root of the problem, I was able to decide that I was good enough, that before the opinion of those around me always comes my opinion and that I am free to do what I want, that I do not need anyone's approval. My approval is enough.

Your turn. Describe how these strong negative events and emotions experienced in childhood now influence your life:

_____
_____
_____
_____
_____

Now, imagine that you were in front of yourself when you were a child, look your inner child in the eyes with compassion and, regardless of the age the child has in your mind, give him a big hug and tell him:

"It's ok, I'm here for you. I love you so much. You are a wonderful child. I am proud of you! You can do anything! ″

Your inner child has gone nowhere, lives in you and needs healing for all the wounds of the past.

We will focus more deeply on this healing process in Awaken Yourself Book 3, after you remember and clearly distinguish who the true "you" is and who this "you" created by society is.

If you take a step back and look at the big picture for a second, the overall scenario for life is so similar and so sad, that it's no wonder why so many people have mental health issues.

Grow up, study, find a job, pay bills, pay taxes... feel miserable and unworthy, as long as you do all this, take some vacations from time to time, to forget about everything you don't like in your life, then retire, die and say you lived.

No, no, no, no, no, no, no!

That can't be called life.

This is NOT life.

This is just a construct that society has subtly iimposed on us and that we have accepted, quietly, while living in silent despair.

Do you want to have the freedom and space to be yourself?

Do you want to have time just to do you?

Wouldn't it be great to be able to experience everything you want to experience? To create? To develop your passions?

Life is what you decide to make of it, not what society dictates you to make of it.

Waking up from social hypnosis is the first step so you can make any change, no matter how small, to what you really want in life.

It's not too late, it's not too early, now is the right time.

Can you accept that more than 90% of everything you think about yourself is not even your truth?

More than 90% of what you think about yourself is the sum of what your parents told you, what your teachers told you, what your society told you, and finally what you started saying to yourself, as a result of the countless interactions with your environment.

You were educated to believe that love is conditioned and you learned this for the first time in your family.

"True love is never conditioned. When love is conditioned, what appears to be love is, in fact, just a subtle manipulation, disguised as love."

- Cristina Joy

"I love you, if you keep quiet.
I love you, if you behave nicely.
I love you, if you're good.
I love you, if you get good grades.
I will buy you the toy you want, if you eat everything from the plate.
I love you, if you graduate from high school.
I love you, if you find a job.
I love you, if.... "

Take a break, close your eyes and let your mind wander among the memories.

See if you can identify a few phrases of conditional love that you heard when you were growing up.

Have you ever heard of such conditions?

Write down some phrases of conditional love that you have heard in your environment:

I love you if:

_____

_____

_____

_____

_____

We've all heard it, whether we remember it or not.

And no wonder we believed them. They just came from the people we loved the most, from the people who took care of us.

It was so easy to accept them.

Have you ever felt the conditions imposed by your parents?

The bigger question is:

Who told them how to behave with you?

No one. They copied what their parents did, their teachers, the society in which they lived at the time.

Who explained to them what is good for the harmonious development of children? No one.

They copied what their parents did, their teachers, the society in which they lived at the time.

If you go down the spiral, can you realize how obsolete are all the things that have been told and passed on to us as truths?

Then, how can everything you have been told in your whole life be relevant and up to date?

It may not be relevant, at least not entirely.

You just accepted everything that was told to you and everything that happened to you, as absolute truths, because, you did not have the conscience and the discernment to separate what is right and what is wrong for you, from everything you lived and everything you have been taught.

You considered everything to be "normal" and this normal has accompanied you all your life, while you thought that there is no other way to think, feel and be.

You forgot what it's like to be unconditionally loved.

It was normal to be loved and celebrated when you did something good. It was normal to be criticized when you did something wrong, without even realizing that mistakes are the only way to learn and that they too must be celebrated. It was normal to complain about money, about its lack, it was normal to complain about absolutely anything, even if that didn't change anything and brought you negative states. It was normal to stop asking questions and being creative at school. Sometimes, even at home.

It was normal to eat whatever you were given, being considered capricious, if you listened to your body, when it rejected a certain type of food.

It was normal to be afraid to be listened to at school, to be afraid to walk the streets alone, to be afraid at home.

It was normal to have teachers screaming at you or hitting you from time to time. Well, you needed education, with good words you didn't understand.

It was normal for children to laugh at you when you took small grades.

It was normal to be harassed if you smelled bad.

It was normal to always be in competition with your colleagues.

It was normal to feel ashamed, embarrassed and guilty when you wanted to help your colleagues with exams.

It was normal to keep your home and school problems to yourself, no one had the time or availability to talk and really ask you how you feel.

It was normal to be labeled poor and pointed at if you didn't have fitted clothes.

It was normal to be categorized as "stupid" and to be ridiculed by your classmates if you were not able to answer the questions the teachers asked you in class.

Have you experienced any of these "normal" things?

This normal has deeply implemented, in our subconscious mind, that this is life.

That everything is conditioned.

You have been taught WHAT to think, instead of HOW to think.

You were discouraged from drawing your own conclusions.

You were given all the tools and information about what to know (just think about how much material you had to learn and recite parroting during your studies), instead of being given all the tools and information you needed to build your own truth.

Our education system has focused more on developing our ability to memorize facts and fictions than on developing our ability to think for ourselves and discover our own personal opinions and truths.

This "normal" that we have experienced is translated today into our operating system or our belief system. Just as a computer has an operating system, so does our life has an operating system installed. Belief system or how I like to caress it, our BS system (Bulls ** t System).

This is our operating system now, that 95% of our Mac Os or Windows. This is the program that is now running against the background of our daily lives, while consciously operating with the remaining 5% of our conscious mind.

This 95% of the BS system is the magic house, where all your automatic negative thoughts come from, like an avalanche.

From that society trash can I was telling you about.

Let's put everything in perspective, so you understand why I think it's important for you to know that.

- Do you know that, on average, we think between 12,000 and 60,000 thoughts a day?

- Do you know that of all these daily thoughts, 80% are negative and 95% of them are repetitive?

Can you see how you create your current reality, based on your past experiences?

Your mind is the "hub" where you constantly rearm doubts, anxiety, lack of self-confidence, lack of self-control, the mentality that what you have is never enough, lack of self-esteem, lack of self-love, the belief that you do not deserve to have everything you want, the lack of compassion for yourself and those around you, any other type of lack.

Obviously, if you rearm them unconsciously, without stopping, now it's easier for you to understand why you always repeat the same patterns, that's why you attract the same type of people around you and why you continue to have the same type of experiences throughout your life, even if, in different places, with different people.

All these negative wonders are gathered in your head, from past experiences, from everything you have lived and all the conclusions you have drawn from your experiences and, whether you want to or not, your negative thoughts and beliefs are always there for you, as a huge family that is always by your side and that rarely leaves you alone.

95% of your behavior comes from the operating system running in the background, which has carefully gathered all the information about who you are from your environment and which has been successfully installed until you became an adult.

This is the foundation that you have built on and that you are building on who you are today.

This is your overflowing cup of tea, from the story of the Zen Master.

Everything you think, everything you say, everything you believe, comes from all past experiences over which you had no control, bundled with the meaning you gave then, based on the understanding you had when you were little.

If all you get from here is the understanding that you are operating from an operating system that is not even yours, you are already waking up to a greater truth and my goal for the first book, from a series of seven, is achieved.

Awakening to another level of understanding is as climbing higher and higher steps on a ladder.

You have to climb the low ones first, in order to develop your confidence that you can climb the ones that seem more difficult, at first sight.

Has the power of unconditional love ever been explained to you? Has anyone taught you kindness and why is it wonderful to show it, not only to acquaintances?

Do you remember any of your teachers explaining to you what acceptance, cooperation, honesty, equality, compassion, trust, hope are?

I hope you're one of the lucky ones.

I have never been told about love, kindness, acceptance, equality, compassion or anything else related to these subjects in primary school, high school or college.

Ah! Sure. I remember!

We were talked about for a few seconds about kindness, when we were asked for money for teachers' gifts, near Christmas or at the end of the year.

And then, how could I have given such gifts to the world, when I was not educated to do so and I was not even educated to think for myself?

The absence of such basic values had so many side effects as I navigated through life.

Do you know where all these experiences automatically direct us?

Towards adopting a victim consciousness that continues to spread ignorance and conditioned love.

The new story that people have begun to tell themselves, without even noticing, sounds something like this:

"Things happen to me and I answer, I defend myself, I have no power over the things that happen to me. I am a victim of the circumstances. "

All this internal conversation made you weak, made you see yourself as the "little me", made you forget what it's like to feel really awake in your own life.

All this has taken you further and further away from the present moment and kept you a prisoner of your own mind, somewhere between the past and the future.

And hasn't it been perpetuated in all our relationships with those around us?

"I love you if you do that."

"I love you, if you bring me this."

"I love you, if you make me feel that way."

"I'll be fine if that happens."

"I'll be happy when...."

With this type of conditioning, it's no wonder you started spending more and more time in your head and less and less time being truly present.

You have always started to think, in all relationships with those around you, if the things you do are enough and if they make you a pleasant, loving person.

You have begun to think of more and more things that you can do or ask for, in order to get these conditional feelings, which the people around you put up for auction for a certain price, gesture, action or thing offered by you.

So who decides who you are?

From today, you!

Leave everything that is known and decide, from the bottom of your heart, what kind of person you want to be. Take a pencil and write as detailed as possible.

"Sometimes deciding who you are is deciding who you'll never be again."

- Cristina Joy

Today I decide who I am.
I am_____

_____

_____

_____

_____

_____

_____

_____

_____

_____

_____

_____

_____

_____

_____

_____

_____

_____

_____

_____

_____

_____

_____

_____

_____

_____

_____

_____

_____

Chapter 6: What filter do you put on reality?

Now let's play a little and see how awake you are, to start building from there.

What does the Map of Consciousness actually want to highlight?

That there are 17 stages of consciousness awakening and 17 energy levels to which it is calibrated.

I like to explain it like this: there are 17 filters that you can put to your reality.

Just like the ones you use on Instagram when you want to give a different light to your photos.

But here, with the help of these filters, you give another light (meaning) to your life, the surrounding events and your feelings. Using this filter, you decide on a subconscious level how good or bad, beautiful or ugly, happy or unhappy are the events that happen to you.

In other words, the filter through which you see your current reality determines whether you are happy or unhappy.

The good part? You can change the filter whenever you want, just like on Instagram, until you find the one you like best.

No two people in the world will see exactly the same things, although they can look at the same things.

The way we see things is given by the accumulation of lived experiences (the garbage can of society, which we talked about earlier) and the unique way you navigate through life, as a result of them.

The Map of Consciousness is an amazing tool created by PHD David R. Howkins, who explains that we are born with a certain level of consciousness and that, hopefully, at some point in our journey here, we want to really understand this game called life, we will want to really understand how it is played, so that we can have fun at every stage and finally win it. I hope that the exposure to this map of consciousness awakens in you the desire to become an aspirant to the escalation of this imaginary ladder of well-being and real spiritual progress.

Everything that is calibrated below the 200 logarithm,

MAP OF CONSCIOUSNESS

	God-view	Life-view	Level	Scale	Emotion	Process	
POWER	Self	Is	Enlightenment	700-1000	Ineffable	Pure Consciousness	**STRONG**
	All-Being	Perfect	Peace	600	Bliss	Illumination	
	One	Complete	Joy	540	Serenity	Transfiguration	
	Loving	Benign	Love	500	Reverence	Revelation	
	Wise	Meaningful	Reason	400	Understanding	Abstraction	
	Merciful	Harmonious	Acceptance	350	Forgiveness	Transcendence	
	Inspiring	Hopeful	Willingness	310	Optimism	Intention	
	Enabling	Satisfactory	Neutrality	250	Trust	Release	
	Permitting	Feasible	Courage	200	Affirmation	Empowerment	
FORCE	Indifferent	Demanding	Pride	175	Scorn	Inflation	**WEAK**
	Vengeful	Antagonistic	Anger	150	Hate	Aggression	
	Denying	Disappointing	Desire	125	Craving	Enslavement	
	Punitive	Frightening	Fear	100	Anxiety	Withdrawal	
	Disdainful	Tragic	Grief	75	Regret	Despondency	
	Condemning	Hopeless	Apathy	50	Despair	Abdication	
	Vindictive	Evil	Guilt	30	Blame	Destruction	
	Despising	Miserable	Shame	20	Humiliation	Elimination	

falls into the category of destructive, supports falsehood and lack of integrity, and everything that calibrates above 200, falls into the category of the creative, supports the truth, integrity and life.

"One does not become enlightened by imagining figures of light, but by making the darkness conscious."

Try this:

Please take a look at the Map of Consciousness and ignore your religious beliefs. I respect them, only that the map is not necessarily related to any religious entity, but to the level of consciousness you are at now, with the filter you put on the experiences in your life.

The lowest level of consciousness is "Shame". At this level, you think that life is miserable, that you are the victim of everything that happens and that you have not the slightest power over your life.

Life happens to you, and you just react. You are the victim of your environment.

This is the free filter that most people use in their daily lives.

The highest level of consciousness is "Enlightenment". At this level, you think you are one with everything that exists, you are one with the whole Universe.

You become pure consciousness, the notion of separation disappears.

This is the pro filter, the one you have to pay for, which all of us can use, but no one wants to pay for, and which makes everything look great. The payment is usually in consistent awareness of our thoughts and emotions and the meaning we give to things in any given moment.

If your aspirations do not go that far, then imagine how would your life look like at the level of Joy, where you are mostly serene, cheerful, grateful, happy, you enjoy all that life has to offer, you feel complete and capable to solve whatever life throws in your way.

This level is also similar with a pro filter, that you have to pay for, with the same focused awareness on your thoughts, emotions and meaning you give to things, but with a free trial period, which I challenge you to try.

When can you experience joy at no cost at all?

A walk in park, a smile from a friend, a moment you remind yourself to be grateful for everything you have and everything you are? Something else?

_____

_____

_____

Now that you have gained a basic understanding of this map of consciousness, choose the level you think you are at now, without thinking too much.

Shake off the ego, the disguised arrogance and the false sense of importance of a "correct" answer. There is no right or wrong. There is only sincerity with yourself, which allows you to build on a solid foundation.

At what level of consciousness on the map does intuition guide you?

Write it here:

_____

Ok, now that you've chosen the level of consciousness you think you are at, I have to tell you something that science supports.

Whatever level you decide you are at, studies say you are two levels below.

I know, I didn't like that either! However, it is important to develop an honest relationship with ourselves if we want to really know who we really are and change in new ways.

Write the real level here:

_____

Studies show that our magical brain will make us see ourselves on a higher than we really are.

If you are determined to improve your quality of life and constantly evolve to a new level of consciousness, then you must understand each level and become an objective observer of your predominant thoughts, emotions and actions.

Only by objectively observing them will you realize what you like and what you do not like in what you do, in the way you behave, in the actions you take or do not take.

I have to tell you that, when I was first exposed to this map, it was quite difficult for me to accept that I am so low on the ladder. After about seven years of self-education and personal development, I was only at the level of "Fear".

Don't get too excited about the fact that you find yourself happy from time to time, we're talking about the level you find yourself predominantly, having as a compass your thoughts, the way you feel most of the time and the place you come from when you take action. Now I am at the level of "Availability" and, I admit, with greater humility, that serious internal work is to be done, in order to advance on the scale of consciousness. Give yourself patience and time to digest everything. As we move forward, everything will make sense.

To be truly aware, write below, without thinking too much, the first answers that come to mind, because they are usually the real ones:

My predominant emotions are:

_____

_____

_____

_____

_____

_____

_____

_____

_____

_____

My predominant thoughts are:

_____

_____

_____

_____

_____

_____

_____

_____

_____

My predominant actions are:

_____

_____

_____

_____

_____

_____

_____

_____

_____

_____

PART 3: HEALING

Chapter 7: Honesty break. What do you really want?

IIf there is something I want you to turn your attention to, in your daily life, that something is the genuine openness, which is hidden in every question and answer, that follows.

Be honest with yourself, really reflect on every question and write the first things that come to mind:

What do I want to achieve here and now?

_____
_____
_____

Why am I trying to awaken? Why do I seek happiness? What is that something that I feel is missing from my life and that pushes me towards evolution right now?

_____
_____
_____

How do I feel most of the time?

_____
_____

How satisfied am I with my life on a scale of 1-10?

1–2–3–4–5–6–7–8–9–10

You probably struggled on your own with the following questions, every time life shot you in the back:

Why am I here?
What is the purpose of my existence?
What is all this for?

Let me free you a little from these difficult questions.

As we delve deeper into these questions, in the following books, for the moment, rest in the following understanding, take a deep breath three times, and allow yourself to notice if you resonate with these statements:

You are a soul having a human experience.

You have chosen to come here, you are not blocked or forced to be here.

You are here to enjoy your own evolution.

Life happens for you to enjoy it.

Your goal here is to feel good, to have fun, to experience everything that can be experienced.

You might say:

"To have fun? I don't see the fun part anywhere!
I work, I work and I work again. Life is a struggle. "

And I'll tell you, whatever your answer, you're right.

"Life can be a prison or a wonderful adventure."

It all depends on how we look at life.

It all depends on the filter through which we choose to see life and the things that happen to us.

To keep everything as simple as possible, let us focus on the idea of "feeling good", let's make the main idea about "well-being", because in this word hides the magical and secret kingdom that everyone pursues with a crazy obsession, in different ways, often without even realize this.

If you have been actively looking to awaken, you probably already know that everything is energy and that everything vibrates at a certain frequency.

If you are not aware of this, it's ok, there are a lot of books, articles and places where you can find detailed information about it.

To simplify everything, imagine that the lowest frequency is the blackest, worst and most negative feeling in the world, the worst feeling you can feel in your body. Let's say it's, for example, a cocktail of hatred, extreme envy, revenge. The highest frequency is the pinkest (because pink is my favourite, haha), brilliant and positive feeling in the world, the most brilliant sensation you can feel in your body. Let's say it's, for example, a cocktail of happiness, extreme joy, ecstasy and gratitude.

As we need a separate book just to get into this in detail, and I am fascinated by this subject and the science behind it, which confirms everything, rest in the understanding that that book will come in a very simple and easy-to-follow language and understand and that all you have to do now is rest your attention in the here and now and align with the idea that well-being is the strongest vibration in the whole Universe. As we are currently experiencing a global pandemic, your awakening to the importance of raising your frequency by prioritizing your well-being is vital.

Why do I say that? Viruses are, like everything else, energy.

And they vibrate at a certain frequency. Obviously they vibrate at a low frequency, sickness, fear, discomfort, negativity. A cocktail of negative sensations that you feel in your body. If you feel good and you are on a high frequency all the time, I wonder if a virus can touch you?

Grasp that for a moment and then open your heart and give yourself the answer that resonates, inside you, as truth.

Please reflect on the following questions and allow your answers to come easily, reminding yourself that there is no right or wrong, good or bad. Nobody judges what you answer. They are your personal beliefs, and when you take them out of your head and put them on paper, you get a clearer vision of how you see, feel and experience life.

What is my ultimate goal in everything I do?

_____

Why do I do everything I do?

_____

Why am I learning?

_____

Why do I work?

_____

Why do I buy beautiful clothes?

_____

Why do I choose beautiful hairstyles?

Why do I choose to travel?

Why do I want to buy a house?

Why, after buying a house, do I want a bigger house?

Why do I get into relationships?

Why do I want / do not want to get married?

Why do I want / do not want to have children?

Why do I want / don't want a family?

Why do I want / do not want to move to another country?

Why do I want / don't want more money?

Why do I want / don't want more material things?

Why do I want / don't want to have friends?

_____

While a million different people will give different
answers, according to their own perception, ask yourself:

What am I really looking for?

_____

Why am I doing all this?

_____

What is the real purpose behind all these actions?

_____

Now, think of a time in your life when you said this or
something similar:
I will be happy when I finish school.
I will be happy when I finish high school.
I will be happy when I move away from my parents.
I will be happy when I finish college.
Oh, I can't wait to finish school, high school, college!

Then you got a job and started saying to yourself:

- I hate this job, I will be happy when I will get a better
job, with more money and more free time. You said that to
yourself, though maybe, you didn't take any action in that
direction.
Let's say you want a house of your own, you work hard
for it, you can make a 30-year mortgage for it, and after
only a month since you've moved in it, you say to yourself:

- This house is a bit small, I don't have enough space. I'll be happy when I buy a bigger house.

You dream of being in a relationship. In the end, you meet the person you think you want, in order for you to be happy.

The first days/ weeks are, just like the fairytales and, after only a month of relationship, you start to tell yourself:

- I would like her/ him to be more attentive to my needs, I would like this person to bring me flowers every day, I would like him/ her to take out the garbage without me asking, I would like him/ her to know what my needs are without having to communicate them, I would like this person to make me really happy.

Here's the trick. Nobody, nobody, nobody, nobody, and when I say nobody, I mean ABSOLUTELY NO ONE, except you, can make you really happy.

It's up to you to know how to be happy.

I know, your brain will lie puzzled reading these lines. Will say:

- What? I work, clean, cook, study, train, pay attention, time, flowers, take out the trash, bring money home and, in addition, I have to make myself happy too?

Yes, that's right.

It all starts with you.

It all starts with the well-being you have create for yourself. It all starts with awareness of your own needs and desires. If you don't know what makes you happy, how can you believe that someone around you will know?

Especially in couples, such awareness is vital for a harmonious relationship. Even if, say, you know what makes you happy and you know how to make yourself happy, if the person next to you does not know what brings them happiness, they will unconsciously blame you for

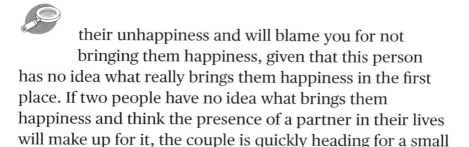their unhappiness and will blame you for not bringing them happiness, given that this person has no idea what really brings them happiness in the first place. If two people have no idea what brings them happiness and think the presence of a partner in their lives will make up for it, the couple is quickly heading for a small or large disaster with reproaches, quarrels and frustrations and will have no idea how they got there.

Try this:

Imagine two unhappy people, who enter into a relationship, to be made happy, to take, to steal energy from each other. How long can this relationship last?

Estimate here:

_____

Imagine two happy people, who enter into a relationship, to amplify together the happiness they already feel, to share with each other, to give, to grow. How long can this relationship last?

Estimate here:

_____

Always remember:

"The way someone treats you has nothing to do with you, but with the way they feel inside."

- Cristina Joy

Now, honestly ask yourself:

What makes me really happy? How can I make myself happy? What moments/ experiences can I create for my happiness? What really makes my soul happy and does not depend on anyone but me?

_____
_____
_____
_____
_____
_____
_____
_____
_____

Everything you have ever done in your life has had the ultimate goal of making you feel good.

The strongest and hidden desire behind everything we do, as human beings, is to be happy, to finally feel GOOD.

Good food, studies, relationships, travel, experiences, friends, parties, careers, family, material things, you name them, because I'll ask you, right after, what is the real reason you did and do all this?

You are constantly looking for the vibe of "feeling good". Or, simply put, you pursue "well-being."

You are after the highest frequency in the Universe.

We are all in a constant search for this feeling.

It's so simple and yet it seems so complicated.

So complicated that this great "secret" prevents us from enjoying this experience called "life" to the fullest, and, most of the time, we don't even realize it.

We have become so good at covering up the real reason behind what we do every day, as if it is an international secret.

It's no big secret.

What is in return? It is a defense mechanism, which you have unconsciously created, to pass the responsibility for your well-being, your happiness and your emotions to the conditions in your environment.

It's super easy to do that, isn't it?

You blame pandemics, government, news, bad luck, family, friends, corporations, the incompetence of others, so others are always responsible for how you feel and you don't have to do anything.

You might say that you are a victim. Thus, it's not your fault.

What can you do? "You little and helpless one."

Just think how many times you said this to yourself:

I'll be happy when all this madness ends.

I will be happy when the government is no longer corrupt.

I will be happy when the problems around me are solved.

I will be happy when my parents help me more.

I will be happy when I am in a relationship.

I will be happy when I get married.

I will be happy when I have children.

I will be happy when I have a job.

I will be happy when I am promoted.

I will be happy when I have a better job.

I'll be happy when I move to another house.

I will be happy when I move to another country.

I will be happy when I travel.

I will be happy when....

And now, to save you from all the madness, for the sake of the idea, let's say that you have successfully obtained them all. Absolutely everything you ever wanted, you have now. Absolutely everything you had on your wish list. Done! Now what?

What's next now? Classic sequel:

I will be happy when I finish my home mortgage.
I will be happy when I can afford an even bigger house.
I will be happy when I am alone.
I will be happy when I have more friends.
I will be happy when I travel further and further.
I will be happy when I no longer have a job, but only a lot of money.
I will be happy when....
Let's say now that you got ABSOLUTELY EVERYTHING you asked for.
ALL. You have the money, you have the job, you have the relationship, you have everything.
Now what?
I tell you. Science proves this.
You will find other reasons to postpone happiness in the future.
Can you see how you always postpone your happiness for the future and how everything you get usually lasts a maximum of a few days?
Have you ever wondered why?
Be honest now, what happens when you finish your home mortgage, when you can afford an even bigger house that you don't need, when you are alone as you wish now, when you have more friends, when you travel even further

and further , when you get money without working, when do you move back to a new country?

Exactly, you are happy for a moment and a half and after that, you return to your favorite pattern. As soon as you achieve what you set out to do and what you thought would bring you that magical happiness, you continue to postpone happiness in the future, again, creating new conditions that must be met for you to be happy.

There is a "bug" in our minds called hedonic adaptation. Our mind is built in a very funny way. It gets bored quickly. Only less than 1% of the world's population is aware of this.

If you leave your happiness in the hands of your mind, chances are that you will never be happy in the long run.

When you get something you want again, you are a little happy, for the moment, while what you have got is new, and then your mind gladly transfers your new thing to the hedonic adaptation folder. Nothing is interesting for your mind after losing its element of novelty.

And then... when are you really happy?

When do you stop to feel really good?

Do you resonate with the idea that all you pursue, in everything you do, is to feel good?

If so, then, with your hand on your heart, answer the question:

If you want to feel good and you think that a new global circumstance, a new government, a new country, a new job, a new house, a new relationship, they will bring you exactly that... if you don't feel good about this global circumstances, with this government, with the country you are in now, with the job you are working in now, with the house you are in now, with the relationship you are in now and you take yourself, with you, no matter where you choose to go in your next experiences, what makes you think you will feel good then and there in the future?

_____
_____
_____
_____
_____

Can you see where I'm going with all this?

Feeling good is what you are looking for, but you have learned to look for it in all the wrong places.

Feeling good is always somewhere in the future.

You look for the "feeling of well-being" in external circumstances, in other people, in other places, in objects.

What this means?

Let's be a little objective and analyze coldly.

If your feeling of well-being, your happiness, depends on external circumstances, other people and the objects you have in your possession, are you not giving on the tray, forever, voluntarily, your power to feel good here and now? In this moment? Unconditional?

To make everything sound even worse (read "more real"), if the source of your feeling of well-being comes from external circumstances, from the presence or absence of other people, from the presence or absence of objects and they can be changed/ taken at any time, doesn't make it obvious that you are always in a bubble of insecurity, in a state of continuous addiction? Doesn't make it true that you have absolutely no control over how, when and how much you will you feel really good/ happy/ safe?

Do you really want your peace and well-being to be so fragile?

Why is this feeling of well-being so important?

Imagine a moment in your life when something doesn't go the way you want it to. Do so, just for the sake of awareness.

How does this translate into a day / week / month / life if you, at any moment of your existence, leave your well-being in the hands of numerous external factors, over which you have not the slightest control?

"When something goes wrong in my Universe, when I receive bad news, when I am rejected, when I don't get what I want, when I have a failure, when I have a bad day, when I am in a bad mood:

My general condition is

_____

Relationships with those around me are

_____

My perspective on life is

_____

The general quality of my life is

_____

I feel

_____

I have the feeling that

_____ "

Be honest, is this life going the way we always want it to be?

_____

When something goes wrong, are you still happy to be alive?

_____

While I am all flower-power and a convinced optimist, I am also very anchored in reality, and the reality of 2020 looked like this:

Suicide. Almost every 20 seconds someone commits suicide in the world, and that means over 1 million souls a year.

Depression. One of the most common mental illnesses. Globally, more than 264 million people of all ages suffer from depression. Depression leads to suicide.

Anxiety. It affects more than 250 million people globally. What is this anxiety and how is it different from depression? Anxiety is an excessive feeling of worry, while depression comes with excessive feelings of hopelessness and lack of values to continue.

Loneliness. Loneliness has reached new heights, reaching millions of people globally, while a deep sense of disconnection is increasingly felt among those who use social media frequently.

Imagine that, globally, millions of people have no one to talk to, no one to share their thoughts, feelings and worries with.

The existence of social networks deepened this feeling of loneliness, as the authentic human connection and human interaction have been replaced with likes, comments, emoticons, gifs and text messages. Now, if we add, like the icing on the cake, the effects of a global pandemic, we will immediately realize that we have more important things to focus on than the misery that is repeatedly promoted in the media.

Wow, can you believe that there are more than half a billion people, globally, who not only don't feel well most of the time, but who are also in constant distress most of the time?

Can you imagine that the numbers can be much higher, given the current global situation?

Can you imagine that all the sad situation of these suffering people is created by one thing, which is in their power of control?

What creates the suffering that comes with anxiety, depression and loneliness?

Excessive negative thoughts that these people constantly think about, without understanding that they can control those thoughts.

Their suffering is not external.

It's not like they fell, they hit one part of their body and now they have pain in that area.

Their suffering is internal.

You don't see it and that makes it dangerous. Everything seems ok with them, from the outside.

All their suffering is caused by the catastrophic thoughts they think, without stopping.

And, what does the media do?

It feeds them more suffering, feeding them daily with exaggerated news, put in a catastrophic way, and, as a result, they further intensify this continuous loop of worry, fear, hopelessness, loneliness.

Can you take a step back and see the big picture?

Can you see that all these people, who are suffering, are affected by the lack of understanding of their own power, to control their thoughts?

Can you see how crazy everything is?

Can you imagine that, in reality, as a result of the daily broadcast, in proportion of over 99%, of completely negative news, the number of people suffering from one of these mental health problems is increasing more and more?

As zen and positive as I am, I can't help but wonder why this attack on global well-being?

Why is information promoted on all TV stations in a way that causes irreparable global suffering?

Let me answer.

People overwhelmed with fear, are people easy to control, manipulate and influence.

That's always been the case.

Don't get me wrong, nobody says for them not to broadcast what they want on TV, they will do it anyway.

I am referring to the WAY this news is disseminated, given that those who coordinate these media have a perfect understanding of how the human mind works and what's the result from the constant consumption of negative information.

Should I add, as a bonus, that social anxiety is amplifying globally?

The collateral damage that this global pandemic, so wonderfully promoted, in every corner of the world, has produced, is perhaps harder to notice, because you will not see anything about it on TV, but it exists and requires our attention.

You don't have to be big to make a difference where you are.

You just have to care.
All you have to ask yourself is:

"What am I pretending not to see?"

_____

_____

_____

There may be great opportunities for you to understand more things, see more things, and even change something around you.

Maybe a person's life, maybe more.

We are in all this madness together.

Although we have been encouraged to look at ourselves as enemies that can make each other sick, the reality is not so.

Humanity in us must not be dissipated, just by a little mediated manipulation. We are stronger than that.

Either we see it or not, we all suffer in the same way inside. After all, we are made of the same "material".

If you help a person around you, even if only by giving them a smile = hope, you are doing an extraordinary job for humanity, as you alleviate a little suffering.

"Suffering, ignorance and indifference are more widespread, more invisible and more harmful than any virus on this planet."

- Cristina Joy

As we awaken, unite and do our bit, by spreading a little hope, where fear is promoted, we will have fewer and fewer people on the side of suffering and mental illness and more motivated people, not just to they remain alive, but also to become the leaders of their own lives and to spread hope, joy and love, further.

Only the unity of humanity can awaken people even more to self-education and cultivating their own well-being, as well as to solving even bigger problems, caused by manipulation, lack of education and lack of critical thinking skills:

- mental health
- child abuse
- domestic violence
- street violence
- verbal violence
- malice and competition for resources
- fear of lack
- the imaginary competition between us

Why do you think all this is happening?

Why do you think people commit suicide? Why do you think people suffer from depression, anxiety, loneliness? Why do people abuse their own children? Why does domestic violence increase even more in "popularity"? Why do you think street violence increases? Why do you think we are becoming worse and more competitive in resources? I can't help but mention the toilet paper beating, since the beginning of the pandemic. Why are we in a constant imaginary competition between us?

Have you ever wondered?

Do you think that people, when they feel good, feel like causing suffering to those around them?

Have you ever heard someone say:

I am so happy, I feel so good, so I think I'm going to kill myself or I think I'm going to hurt someone today? Nope!

Can you objectively observe how important well-being is in human existence?

Can you see what a negative overall effect the absence of well-being can have?

When people feel good, they don't feel like taking their own lives.

When people feel good, they don't feel like being violent.

When people feel good, they don't feel like hurting anyone.

When people feel good, they can easily see the good parts of themselves and those around them.

When you feel good, you want to make those around you feel good too.

Just imagine how open, cheerful and uplifting you are with everyone around you, when you feel good.

When you feel good, you don't feel like complaining about everything that is not going well in the world. You feel like rolling up your sleeves and moving on to build, around you, the world you want to live in.

When you feel good, it's easy to wake up your conscience and attention, to notice the negative impact that the different broadcast news has on you, with events, which, anyway, you can't control.

When you feel good, in fact, you don't even have time for such news. All you want is to still feel good and to keep this feeling good, as much as possible.

When you feel good, you are truly AWAKENING.

When you feel good, it's you, in your natural state.

When you feel good, it's you, the one in love with life.

When you feel good, it's you, really alive.

When you feel good, it's you who is grateful for everything.

When you feel good, it's you, the blessed one.

When you feel good, it's you, the compassionate one.
When you feel good, it's you, the one full of kindness.
When you feel good, it's you, the one full of empathy.
When you feel good, it's you, the generous one.
When you feel good, it's you, a force for good.
When you feel good, it's you, happy, here and now.
When you feel good, it's you, the one who is confident that you have the strength to succeed in everything you set out to do.

More important than anything, is that, contrary to what you have been taught to believe, in fact, it is really easy to feel good.

It all starts here and now, with a decision to keep yourself in a constant state of well-being, in a state where you consciously choose to feel good, no matter what happens around you.

Read with your heart:

MY STATEMENT OF AWAKENING TO LIFE

Starting today, ..., I declare with my hand on my heart that the most important thing in my life is my well-being.

Starting today, I choose to live my life with my eyes open.

I choose to be AWAKEN at every moment of my life.

I choose not to take anything as absolute truth and to educate myself to think for myself. I choose to accept everything as it is.

I choose to love all people as they are.

I choose to be kind to those around me, even when they are bad, because now I understand that people are bad with other people when they don't feel good.

I understand now that if I don't feel good about myself, I can't help other people feel good.

I understand that if I'm not happy, I have nothing to offer others.

I understand I can't pour from an empty glass.

I understand that I cannot give love to others if I do not love myself.

I understand that I can't accept other people if I don't accept myself.

I understand that I will never be able to give compassion and empathy until I offer them to me first.

I understand that I will not be able to truly forgive the mistakes of others until I first forgive my own.

I understand that if someone asks me for ten oranges, I can't give them ten oranges unless I go and buy ten oranges.

I understand and accept that I can't give what I don't have first.

I understand that if I choose to feel good only when the circumstances in my life are as I think they should be, I condemn myself, for life, only to temporary and random moments of happiness, unconsciously promoting and perpetuating my state of unhappiness.

I understand that I create happiness and unhappiness through the thoughts I think.

Today, here and now, I declare that I deserve to be happy and that I will make this a priority so that, later, I can give something to the world around me.

Date: .... Signature: ....

Chapter 8: FEAR. To run or to face it?

I had the window wide open, and the title of this chapter was already written. I was getting ready to talk to you about fear. About what it really is and how to get rid of it. I didn't get to type any letters, because a huge bee came into my home through the window. I don't know exactly what it's called. It's like a bee, but ten times bigger.

The first reaction?

My heart skipped a beat! Fear settled in my chest, and without time to think consciously, my subconscious instantly decided that the bee was a danger to me, probably associating countless times when I was stung by bees, wasps, and other relatives of theirs and the countless swellings I had on my face, hands, feet, neck, ears, and who knows what other parts of my body that I don't remember now.

What can I say? I really enjoyed life in the countryside.

I took a deep breath, realized that fear was playing me, and I got up to calmly guide Mr. Bee towards the exit.

When it comes to fear, we always have two options:

1. To react compulsively (unconsciously). I could have stayed in a state of panic, I could have put my body under huge stress for nothing, screaming and running around the house like crazy, hoping that my visitor, Mr. Bee, confused by the noise, will come out voluntarily.

2. To react calmly (aware). I realized that fear is given by the association with other past experiences and worries for the future. In all past experiences, everything has been resolved, every time. What was the worst thing that could happen? To sting me. So what? It stung me many times before and it was ok. So why should I be afraid? Okay,

maybe Mr. Bee was extra special, because he's from London. And yet, I found no real reason for fear. I widely opened the window and started talking to Mr. Bee. I explained that I want to keep writing, that I will tell you about his visit, and that he would do me an enormous favor, if he came out, willingly. Mr. Bee, like a real gentleman, after hitting the glass with full speed few times (yikes!), left the premises.

The lesson?

Fear lies to us, most of the time.

The fears we do not face become our limits.

To be brave does not mean not to feel fear, but to look fear in the eyes and tell it to step aside from the path of your dreams.

Fear will always be there, and our strength is in learning to act in its presence.

Stronger than anything is to realize that fear does not exist in the past (you have already lived it, what it was, it was), nor in the present (when you are truly present, everything is good here and now, you have no real reason to fear), but only in the future.

In other words, the you in the here and now, in this present moment, catastropheses all sorts of future scenarios, which most certainly will not happen. Just how I instantly catastrophized when I saw Mr. Bee in the same room as me.

Even crazier is that we put our bodies under huge stress, even when we watch the news.

What happens when you look at the news?

Your body is in the same place, but your mind is leaving, "on vacation", in the future, and, imagines how all the negative scenarios you heard on the news will become reality.

Tell me honestly, ok?

If we feel fear, most of the time, when we make scenarios for the future, isn't it appropriate then to understand it and to make friends with it?

If here, in the present moment, everything is good and beautiful, but we feel fear isn't it then advisable to give ourselves a little time to develop a friendly relationship with fear?

When we go through a period of instability, we fear for what is to come.

When we know we have a test, an exam or an interview, we feel fear when we think about the result.

In those moments, we don't even realise, and after everything passes, what we don't do is look back and see if we've learned anything from it. Was the fear justified? Did fear tell us the truth or did it make a fool out of us?

Panic and fear can be solved on the spot by simply practicing this easy technique. It's called PAUSE. It helps a lot. Do you feel scared? PAUSE. Stop the mental dialogue and become aware. All you have to do is turn your attention to how you breathe and make sure you breathe deeply. If you close your eyes when you do this, the effect is guaranteed. Try it now and see it for yourself!

Although it is only a short-term solution, it helps a lot.

Imagine waking up one night and the smoke detector alarm goes off. It warns you of a potential fire. Right away, you're scared. It's normal. You smell smoke, you gather your family and you evacuate the house. That's the fear at work. It also has its purpose. It can save our lives.

But what if, after hearing the alarm, instead of quickly assessing the situation and taking the next logical steps, you removed the batteries from the alarm and went back to sleep without checking anything?

As you can already imagine, the problems would have intensified.

However, this is exactly what we do with fear.

Instead of assessing the situation and responding accordingly, we reject and abandon the situation.

Let's say you have a serious problem with your partner, but you feel afraid to face him / her.

Instead of sitting still and talking openly about what is happening (extinguishing the fire) or even calmly come to the conclusion that it is no longer okay to be together. (Getting everyone out of the house, calmly and safely), you pretend everything is ok. (while fire destroys everything)

When we reject fear, our problems are amplified.

They get bigger and bigger, up to a point, when we are forced to solve them.

When we face fear - we sit, we talk, we face fire, we have difficult conversations - we become stronger as a result.

It is very important to understand why we are really afraid.

What lies behind that fear?

 What is really hiding behind that fear?

In order to understand and make friends with your own fear, it is important to invest some time in it.

You have to look at everything, with a child's curiosity.

You have to give yourself time and space, to observe each situation, detached.

Allow yourself to discover what triggers fear, what fear is, in each situation, and to identify what is the best thing you can do to move forward in spite of it.

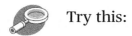 Try this:

Step 1: Think about a fear you felt recently. It can be related to anything. **Write in down:**

_____

Step 2: Find a quiet place where no one will bother you and close your eyes.

Step 3: Ask yourself: WHY AM I REALLY AFRAID?

Ask yourself - Why am I really afraid? What is behind my fear? Why am I really afraid?

Keep asking yourself, until you feel that the answers become clearer, deeper and closer to the truth.

Write down all the answers that come to mind.

_____
_____
_____
_____
_____
_____
_____
_____
_____
_____
_____
_____
_____

Let's say you go to an interview for a job.

You feel paralyzed and afraid. You think you won't get it.

You start to wonder - Why am I really scared?

Let's say that the first answer that comes to mind is: insecurity. You are afraid that you will not succeed, that you will not have a job and a stable income. You are afraid of uncertainty.

You ask yourself again - Why am I really afraid?

The next answer that comes to mind: self-esteem. You are afraid that you are not good enough, qualified enough, prepared enough.

You ask yourself again - Why am I really afraid?

The next answer that comes to mind - family and friends will think I'm a loser. You are afraid of the opinion of others.

You notice now that the fear that appears on the surface may have a totally different motivation than the fear that you actually feel in the depths of your being.

This question helps you understand your fear.

Now let's make friends with fear.

In the example above, I found that the fear of not getting a job is actually the fear of the opinion of the people around you.

As soon as you discover the real fear, you need to ask yourself:

What is the worst thing that can happen?

_____

_____

_____

_____

_____

Let's say you don't get that job and your friends, family, etc. will laugh at you.

And so?

Is that reason enough not to try your luck? Obviously not!

What do you have to do to be a comrade, for life, with any fear that comes your way?

To accept the worst scenario that can happen, and to realize that it's not such a big deal.

How did I overcome my fear of heights? I did Sky Diving.

1. I wondered why I'm scared? Why am I really afraid? The answer, totally predictable, death.

2. I wondered, "What's the worst thing that can happen?" To die. The parachute won't open and that's it.

3. I became aware of the fear, accepted the worst scenario and jumped.

You're going to say I'm crazy, I'm looking for trouble and so on.

That's what I would have said about myself a few years ago. Not now.

What I discovered to be true for me was that until I overcame my fear of death, I did not really begin to live.

"Fear does not stop death, it stops life."

As in most scenarios, fears are actually a kind of soap opera in our head, which does not happen in real life, but which put a brake on the most daring desires and which stop us from experiencing life to its true potential.

Personally, I grew up believing that fear is something bad, that when I feel fear I have to step aside, hide, run away and not go in the direction where fear is more oppressive.

Until I evolved and realized that fear is one of the best emotions we can have.

Fear is the bridge between what we are now and what we want to become.

We grow when we feel fear and act in spite of it.

You'll say:

- Yeah, you're right, but it's damn uncomfortable.

And I will say:

- Yes, that's right.

If it's not uncomfortable, you don't grow, and if you don't grow... you go, slowly and surely, to what I like to call spiritual suicide.

You are here to experiment, to grow, to overcome challenges and not to run away from them.

I used to run, to cancel, to avoid, to hide, every time an event, a situation or a certain thing made me feel afraid.

Until one day, when I overcame a huge fear: the fear of flying.

But, don't imagine that I went through it like everyone else, by booking a plane ticket and flying like a zen queen to a certain destination.

I did it at the extreme level.

It was somewhere, about 12 years ago, when, blindfolded, in a competition that focused on overcoming limits, I was challenged to (obviously) exceed my limits.

I had accepted the challenge of overcoming my fear of heights, without knowing what I was getting into and what I had said 'Yes' to, so easily.

I remember, like yesterday, how I got into the car, blindfolded and, with a heavy heart, trying to figure out where the car was going.

The whole action took place in Bucharest, and I knew every alley, maybe better than the most accurate GPS.

I tried to take into account every turn of the car and every traffic light stop, to realize where I was going.

According to my calculations, I was already on my way out of Bucharest, to Clinceni. In Clinceni I knew that there was an aerodrome and planes. I thought to myself "No way!" and I was secretly hoping that I had miscalculated and was still in Bucharest.

The car stopped, I felt a lump in my throat and I was looking forward to finding out where I am and what I am going to do.

When they took off the bandana from my eyes, I started to tremble from all my wrists, as soon as I realized that I was in front of an acrobatic plane, which was ready to fly.

After it was explained to me that I would do acrobatics, in the air, with that old plane, I was asked, again, if I still keep my yes for this challenge.

I could refuse, but despite my uncontrollable fear, something in me pushed me to say yes.

A few minutes later, I regretted my decision. I was on the plane, ready to take off, just me, my fear and the pilot.

The takeoff was uncomfortable and full of adrenaline, but the fear of my life was just about to come.

As soon as we reached the optimum altitude, the plane began what it was scheduled to do.

Acrobatics.

Also I must underline that the plane was an old model and there was no seat belt.

Instead of a seat belt, it actually had a sort of horse harness. A harness in which you were caught, in case of something, not to "pour" yourself too hard.

Now let me explain to you what happened, through the eyes of a person stiff with fear.

The plane was constantly turning upside down, and I was practically hanging like a terrified bat. Few seconds later we were spiraling toward the ground, as if we were about to crash.

I felt like my heart was overwhelmed with fear, that it was going to explode, that it was going to crack.

"I've been this far," I said to myself.

I must add that every time the plane rolled over, I hung upside down in a wonderful harness and that all sorts of dead insects from the plane came to my face. You should have seen how tight I kept my mouth shut. I was afraid the insects could get in my mouth. You can laugh, it's fine, but I was really terrified.

Bonus, the plane's window was caught in a nut that I had been warned would open the entire roof of the plane if I accidentally touched it.

I've lived through the most awful tens of minutes of my life. At least, that's what I thought then.

With all the fear, at first, I really thought:

- Wow, what a beautiful view!

That was in the first seconds, when the plane reached the necessary altitude to start the acrobatics.

What followed was full of shock and horror, I must admit.

With every second, I could see my death even more clearly.

I sat with a small heart, like a ball and waited for something to happen, at any moment.

But obviously it was all in my head.

Right near the end of the madness, something in me has changed.

Fear turned into curiosity.

I had already seen that nothing happened when we spiraled lightly towards the ground, and the pilot had unconsciously won my vote of confidence.

Suddenly, I felt safe, and not even hanging in the harness, when the plane was upside down, didn't bother me anymore.

The dead insects that came to my face?

I ignored them and amused myself with such a playful attitude, that you might say it wasn't true.

As I was saying, somewhere, I don't know exactly when, a click occurred.

Had the hedonic adaptation been what I was experiencing? Had my brain got used to the experience?

It is certain that, at some point, I put my fear aside and began to enjoy the flight itself.

I still remember when, after all the acrobatics, the pilot asked me in my helmet if I was okay.

I was so fascinated by all the sensations, the view and with how much nonsense I hung in the harness, gracefully avoiding the dead insects that came upon me, every time the plane rolled, that I could not even hear the pilot. It was as if he was somewhere in another scenery talking to someone else.

I was so, in a state of zen (read shock), that I didn't even realize he was talking to me.

When I reached the ground, well, I was shaking from all my wrists, the adrenaline was bubbling through all the cells of my body and I couldn't believe that I had escaped alive from all this experience.

The adrenaline and the joy of getting out of this safe and sound on the ground were a very strange and new combination for me.

All this experience aroused in me an enormous curiosity, a desire to experience more of the things that terrify me.

I realized how many things I missed because of the fear and the mental scenarios I was doing.

For the last eleven years, I've been flying a lot, I've had all kinds of activities that scared me, from befriending dangerous animals, to giant swings, with a huge precipice below - in Bali, causing avalanches and lerning survival techniques - in the mountains, until rappelling down a super tall building.

However, it was something I had not done and longed for.

I was curious if, after so many years of facing fear, I would feel afraid to do sky diving.

I was super curious to see how I would feel when I jumped off the plane.

So, I chose this activity as a gift from me, for me, for my birthday.

It was just between me and me and I didn't tell anyone what I was planning to do, not even to my close friends.

I felt it was just between me, myself and I.

In addition, I felt that if I announced acquaintances, all I would do was worry them. When, all I wanted was to enjoy the experience freely, without remorse that I caused panic in others, even though I was the one who, in theory, should have panicked.

It was Saturday morning, September 5, 2020, at 6:30 a.m. and, after incredible efforts, the night before, to find a car available for a morning ride, I was riding zen in a taxi, somewhere in March, a small town in the Uk.

I was ready to go to the North London Sky Diving Center, which is somewhere in the field, about a 20-minute drive from March.

Registration for Sky Diving started at 8 am, but I wanted to be among the first, because, at the center, you jump in the order in which you get to the registration. There is no hourly schedule.

I got there as number 7, and 10-15 minutes after I got there, the queue became huge.

In the queue, I discovered a lot of people, of all ages, who had come on other occasions, but who, due to the wind, could not jump with the parachute.

For safety reasons, there are strict conditions. The team there puts your safety first, and if the wind is not favorable, it does not fly.

And no, they don't care if you give negative reviews or if you insist.

They must respect the safety measures, especially since it is not only about your life and safety, but also about the instructor who jumps with you.

As I had seen that the wind was favorable in the morning, I was so excited to be able to experience Sky Diving for the first time and it was as if I felt that everything will be alright and that it would jump.

The registration started and we did the training in which we were explained very clearly what we have to do. (not much, to be honest)

Basically, you have to follow the instructions of the instructor you jump with.

When you are ready to jump, you have to keep your head on your back, keep your hands on the harness and release your hands as soon as the instructor taps you on the shoulder.

The next step was getting equipped. It seemed like the enthusiasm grew for everyone. So did the tension.

I noticed, with curiosity, that I had a state of deep peace, from the moment I arrived, until I got on the plane.

The people there asked me how I felt, and all that came naturally to me, with a unexplainable calm, was: "I can't wait to jump!"

It was time to board the plane, and the same unexpected calm was still present in me.

It was as if I was going to the club to have fun, not at a frightening altitude, to jump out of the plane.

On the plane, at one point, for safety reasons, the crew opens the door to ventilate.

I have to tell you that the -4 degrees, were felt as -20 when the door of the plane opened, during the flight, for the few seconds of ventilation.

Although my instructor and I were number 7, in the order of the registration, the way we were placed on the plane actually made us number 1. That was a real surprise. I felt it as a birthday present from the Universe.

Yeah! Enthusiasm grew stronger and stronger and was strengthened by the trembling of all the joints, caused by the cold.

I analyzed with an extraordinary calm what I felt at every step of the experience and I smiled, with delight, to realize what a huge evolution I have reached in eleven years of "practice" of uncomfortable situations.

I told myself to pay attention to how I feel when I jump, to see if I'm scared.

I was in an extraordinary enthusiasm, I could not wait to jump, and when we were preparing to jump, when my legs hung in the air and I was on the edge of the plane, I had a feeling of peace, hard to describe in words.

As if, in my heart, I knew it was time to do that and push my mental limits. In those moments, the fear ceased to exist. Maybe, fed up with so much defiance, fear

had grown tired of following me and had given me a break. Fear had completely left my mind and body. I was really ready to enjoy the experience.

As soon as I jumped, I was surprised to find that I was breathing harder (which is normal, by the way, but I hadn't been warned about and hadn't thought about, no matter how logical it was).

Few seconds after, I adapted to the pressure and boom, the free fall seemed so natural to me, as if I had done this since I knew myself. In the joy of the experience, I began to look at the parachutist who had jumped in front of us and was filming us. It was great to meet other free falling people in the air.

I felt like my jaws were coming off, but it was a new and funny feeling. In my mind, I saw myself in the style of Crazy Frog. Ring ding ding ding. Hahaha.

When the instructor opened the parachute, it was an even more fun feeling, as if an air balloon was speeding us up.

It was like when you swing, but in a huge aerial swing, with the ground as a view.

The feeling was incredible and one of my favorites.

After opening the parachute, a period of empty dive followed.

A feeling of peace, of zen, of pure joy.

I wanted the feeling of coming down to last as long as possible.

I felt like I was really flying.

The landing was smooth and with clear indications: legs stretched forward, to the sign of the instructor, when I had to put them on the ground. Whatever I say in words is too little compared to how you really feel when you do Sky Diving.

The parachute jump was an experience, which made me realize how much I evolved and at what level I turned the fear, which I felt, into something I look forward to experiencing with curiosity and enthusiasm.

We all have fears, some smaller, some bigger.

If you limit your life and stumble over them, I tell you with my hand on my heart, that you are wasting everything that is most beautiful in life.

Fear is what will block you from progressing, evolving, getting to where you want to be, if you let it overwhelm you.

After more than eleven years of challenges, to make friends with my fear, I can tell you now, with my hand on my heart, that every time you want to do something and fear gets in your way, all you have to do is look fear in the eye, clarify why you are really afraid, and say:

"Fear, move, you're in my way!"

Think about everything you lose every time you give strength to your fear.

Is it worth it? I'm sure it's not.

What can you do? Exactly what I did.

Look fear in the eye and face it, don't run!

The most beautiful things happen when you have the courage to face your fears.

Don't think now that I'm telling you that if you have any fear, no matter how small, for example fear of heights, jumping with a parachute directly is the next logical step, although today's Cristina would do just that.

It's all about taking small steps to conquer it.

"In order to live an extraordinary life, you have to become comfortable with feeling uncomfortable."

- Cristina Joy

Fear makes us feel uncomfortable, we want to avoid it, but when, instead of running away from the uncomfortable, as most people choose to do, and we open our hearts to explore this uncomfortable, a new world is born within us, with us and for us. A new world full of possibilities.

 Try this:

Become a friend with a fear of yours. Answer honestly and use the following questions with confidence, whenever you want to understand a fear you have.

1. What am I afraid of?

_____

_____

2. What is the worst thing that can happen?

_____

_____

3. Am I ok with the worst thing that can happen?

_____

_____

4. How can I explore this fear?

_____

_____

5. What activity/ experience would help me overcome
    this fear?

_____

_____

And, without thinking too much, take action.
The rewards you receive when you face your fear are
extraordinary, but they are only available to the brave.

And you?

What fears have you already overcome?

_____

_____

What other fears do you want to overcome?

_____

_____

I have learned that being brave does not mean not
experiencing fear, but developing a power over it. You don't
have to be fearless to be brave, but you have to be brave to
constructively direct your fear towards the results that
would otherwise prevent you from achieving them.
    I remind you that fear will never completely disappear,
all you have to do is explore it, get to know it and learn to
act, despite it.

To be able or not to be able to achieve things you are afraid of, depends only on you and the conversations you have, you with yourself.

So, come on!

Start conversations full of encouragement with yourself!

With strength and boldness, to new adventures!

Inhale courage, exhale fear.

Fear kills more dreams than failures will ever kill.

"Life is found in the dance of the deepest desires and the greatest fear."

- Tony Robbins

Moment of truth.

Why is it important for you to face your fears? What will you lose if you don't face your fears? What opportunities will you miss?

_____
_____
_____
_____
_____
_____

Chapter 9: How to Connect to the Source of Joy?

If there's one thing I've heard all my life, it's:

Joy, what are you eating? Where do you get so much energy from? Give me some of your energy! How can you be so positive? Why do you smile all the time? I want to be so happy too! I want to smile too! Give me some of your joy!

And I, like a gazelle, reach out to them, palms wide open, and say to them, in a very serious tone:

Take it! Take it! Take it!

I mean, I'm open to giving energy and I'm aware that my presence has the power to change the mood of a person or of a group of people, but what they don't realize is that I'm not always by their side and they fall into the same trap I have spoke earlier. You depend on someone as a source of joy, energy, good cheer, zest for life, and so on.

That person is leaving and you are still unhappy.

So, instead of trying to connect to someone else's source of joy, choose to learn how to connect with your own source of joy.

This journey called life consumes a lot of time and energy.

You agree?

Your emotional journey, if it had a purpose, would be to make sure your soul smiles more.

We tend to take life too seriously. Don't we?

"Calm down! Calm down! Calm down! "

Dear people, good friends, family, co-workers, people around me have told me that.

And me, myself and I, in my mind:

"What's wrong people? I'm very calm. "

Well, I was, just in my own hectic way.

"Calm down! Calm down! Calm down!

Why do you work so hard? Why do you never stop?
Where do you run so fast?

"Calm down! Calm down! Calm down!"

I heard the message over and over again.

I didn't even wonder once, why more people around me were telling me that.

And those words certainly didn't help me calm down. Not at all. On the contrary.

Why?

Because I heard them, but I didn't listen to them.

I didn't take their meaning seriously.

Maybe I was doing this because, even though everyone around me was saying these words to me, they weren't great examples to follow either.

We all ran, like zombies, towards something, it's only that we didn't know towards what.

Subconsciously, we hoped to find happiness or run away from the emptiness and unhappiness that resounded when we really calmed down even for a second, from the marathon of our lives.

Looking at it with my soul and humbly digesting the true meaning of these words, I declare with my hand on my heart that this is the message that helped me enjoy life more and not make a big drama out of nothing, regardless of whether it is a global pandemic, I just lost my plane or failed miserably again at something new.

"Calm down! Calm down! Calm down!
Don't worry about everything that happens!"

Can you control what's going on?

Nope! That was always my sincere and confused answer, as I realized how much I had spent my whole life for things that were, in fact, never under my control. Who said life has to be about suffering?

No one. We have only been given and are given some discreet signs, to incline, unconsciously, to suffering.

We are helped, successfully, as if from all sides, to provoke our suffering, through what we think. The reality?

Life is suppose be fun!

We tend to make big deal out of everything, take everything too seriously, easily build a drama out of any subject, as if we are highly paid drama directors and drama actors, at the same time. The paycheque? Unconscious suffering caused by ourselves, to ourselves.

"Yes, take all the challenges and all the problems I have, Cristina, and after that, I calm down too!"

I feel like someone very upset is blowing in the back of my head as I type.

That's the trick.

Answer me this:

Is it easy to feel good when everything is going well?

Obvious.

What I challenge you to do is to defy everything you have been taught and to feel good when things are not going so well.

Why?

No matter how determined you are to be upset and stressed, you still can't create a solution with the same mentality that created the problem.

To give **Albert Einstein** all due respect:

"We can't solve our problems with the same level of thinking that created them."

The only way we can really overcome the problem is when we manage to get a fresh perspective in thinking and approach.

In other words, tell me what do you do, automatically, when you have a problem?

Are the first thoughts you have positive or negative?

Most of the time negative, probably.

If what you think about the problem is negative, can you find a positive solution?

No, unless you are a genius who succeeds in defying all the laws that exist in the Universe.

No man has been able to find a positive solution to a problem by thinking negatively.

It turns out that if you want to solve a problem without subscribing to the discomfort and suffering that comes with it, you must consciously choose to change the story that you tell yourself about that situation.

In short, I have a problem.

Instead of constantly repeating that I have a problem and suffering because I have a problem - negative mental attitude - I consciously choose to change my story.

I choose to say to myself:

I have a "challenge" - and to ask myself: "How can I solve this challenge?" - positive mental attitude.

As soon as you change the story, you will notice how the discomfort disappears, and the enthusiasm to solve this challenge is born.

All you have to do is change your approach.

In other words, you made a leap in consciousness, in your thinking.

From the level of FEAR - thinking with fear, to the level of COURAGE - thinking with courage.

You have jumped from a lower level of consciousness to a higher level of consciousness.

What do you need to remember from all of this?

That only when you climb, at least one step, to another level of consciousness, can you find answers and solutions to your challenges. All you have to do is learn to ask the right questions. The best solutions come from the best questions you ask.

Some questions that I use when I have challenges and that work every time:

What's good about that?

What can I learn from this situation?

How can I grow out of what is happening?

What limits can I exceed on this occasion?

What other ways to solve this challenge have I not tried yet?

If I were my own coach to find great solutions, what advice would I give myself in this situation?

Which person who went through this can I ask for a fresh perspective?

What is the easiest way to solve this challenge?

If I were the smartest person on Earth, how would I solve this situation?

We will delve deeper and deeper into these ideas in the following books, but for the time being, let us lay a simple, solid foundation that is as easy to understand as possible.

If despair made you go into debt, do you think that by remaining in a state of despair you will get out of debt?

Do you agree that when you feel good, you are more inclined to find solutions?

Obviously.

The big challenge is this:

How do you feel good when everything around you seems to be falling apart?

How can you plug yourself to joy, no matter what?

By setting yourself up to think better thoughts about the situations you notice!

"Your mind will always believe everything you say to it. Nurture it with courage, truth, love. "

It is easy and comfortable to believe that thoughts come and go and that we have no control over them.

The reality is that we are the ones who observe the thoughts, and the thoughts can be controlled.

Thought control training is like gym training.

It gets easier and easier as you practice.

The first step is to become more aware of the thoughts you think about every day.

"You are not a prisoner of your thoughts. You have the ability to control what you think."

- Deepak Chopra

 Try this:

Write daily, for a month, in a diary, the most negative

thoughts you can become aware of every day.

Every day, after you finish writing down the negative thoughts, write down the positive thoughts you can consciously replace them with.

I think over 99% of the world's population is unaware that they can control their thoughts.

What does the vast majority of the world's population do?

Let the thoughts gravitate towards them and accept every thought as true.

Hence the root of suffering, globally.

If you do not consciously choose to control your mind, your mind will control you.

"What consumes your mind controls your life."

Here's how the whole thing works for the majority of the population of this globe:

Step 1 - Something happens.

Step 2 - They notice that something happened.

Step 3 - They have an emotional response to that something, given what they think, what they notice.

Step 4 - If what they notice is something positive, the reaction is positive.

Step 5 - If what they notice is negative, not only will the reaction be negative, but from there, they will perpetuate even more negative thoughts, causing even more suffering.

After reaching step 5, our dear earthlings, resume from the beginning, step 1, to infinity.

"Connecting to joy begins with developing the discipline to control your thoughts. If you don't control what you think, you can't control how you feel and what actions you take. "

- *Cristina Joy*

Think about this:

Global pandemic.

You are constantly bombarded with news that things are getting worse.

You are informed that millions of people have lost their jobs.

To feel empathy and compassion for those people is perfectly human. The challenge is that from such news, a new series begins in your head.

Program installed: Drama.

Let's take the following scenario:

You are lucky, you still have a job, a house, a wonderful family, you are healthy, you also have some savings, which insure you for a few years even if you lose your job, but as soon as you are implanted with this scenario, you start thinking, day and night, about all kinds of dramatic scenarios:

What if I lose my job?

What if I get sick?

What if I lose everything?

What if I don't have anything to eat?

What if, what if and what if all the negative things come to me?

The outcome? You live in an induced state of fear and you need an external stimulus to feel joy. At least, that's what you think.

The real challenge?

Dear soul, while thinking all these things 95% unconsciously, you have successfully installed anxiety in your body, and your immune system begins to deteriorate, as a natural response to the stress caused by the thoughts you have.

All this although, you are at home, you're cozy, you are fine and you have no problem.

Doesn't that sound like you're constantly torturing yourself for an imaginary scenario?

What exactly is **depression?**

Stress caused by negative thoughts about past events, which you keep repeating on the mind screen.

What exactly is **anxiety?**

Stress caused by negative thoughts about future events, which you keep repeating on the screen of the mind.

You know what's funnier (please read "sad")?

You can't change the past scenario, no matter how depressed you choose to be, and all those future scenarios that you are contemplating, most of the time, don't even happen.

This past and future scenarios are just stealing from you this wonderful gift that life has given us and that we neglect more and more: the present moment.

What is this magic with the present moment, which most of us forget to live?

Simple: everything is fine here and now.

You read these lines and everything is fine.

You're ok. You're fine. Everything is fine in your world.

Millions of people on this planet would give anything to be in your place.

You?

You take everything for granted, you don't appreciate that you are fine now and you worry unnecessarily about what was announced on TV, you worry unnecessarily for a tomorrow, over which you have absolutely no control.

The lack of understanding of how our mind works and the fact that we let news, events, random thoughts so easily take control of how we experience life at any time is what causes a lot of misery and suffering, globally.

That causes suffering.
This causes depression.
This causes anxiety.
That causes uncertainty.
That causes stress.
This causes the immune system to weaken.
This makes you more prone to illness.

Science gives us some details, which I hope will broaden your horizons of understanding.

Every single day, we think, on average, between 12.000 and 60.000 thoughts.

What is important to remember is that:

80% of thoughts are automatically negative and 95% of them are repetitive.

I invite you to read again, with your full awareness:

80% of your thoughts are automatically negative and 95% of them are repetitive thoughts.

Is it then vital for you to learn how to control your thoughts?

Obvious!

The thoughts you think can build or demolish you from the ground up.

Thoughts can bring you to the heights of happiness or the heights of despair.

Thoughts can keep you healthy and with a strong immune system. Thoughts can weaken your immune system, while they can seduce you to anxiety, depression and suffering.

As 80% of your thoughts are automatically negative, no matter how positive you are and 95% of them are repetitive, no matter how conscious you think you are, if you do not take the helm and consciously insert positive thoughts, I can easily predict your life.

So many things are happening globally, and we have no control over them.

What can we control?

What we think about what happens. Our strength is in the emotional reaction we have to what is happening.

What do you choose? Do you choose to dwell, by default, on suffering or do you choose, consciously, to dwell on joy?

I challenge you to write on a piece of paper and to put the following statements somewhere in your eyesight:

My thoughts become my emotions.
My emotions become my actions.
My actions become the results I get.

"Watch your thoughts, they become words; watch your words, they become actions; watch your actions, they become habits; watch your habits, they become character; watch your character, for it becomes your destiny."

- Lao Tzu

And now, let's have a moment of awareness.

Try this:

If my thoughts are negative and my emotions are negative, my actions are: ....

If my thoughts are positive and my emotions are positive, my actions are: ....

Therefore, I want my predominant thoughts to be: ....

Magic begins to happen the moment you decide to prioritize your well-being.

True magic begins when you decide that, no matter what happens in your world, you will consciously choose to stay in a state of calm and power. True magic continues when you choose, at any time, consciously, the thoughts you are thinking.

Your life completely changes when you choose to consciously create your own joy and stay connected to it no matter what happens around you. I know, it's a challenge, but I promise you, when you get connected to your own joy, no external event will be able to shake your inner peace.

"Happiness is a choice. Nothing will make you happy until you choose to be happy. No one will be able to make you happy unless you decide to be happy. Your happiness will not come to you. It can only come from you. "

- Ralf Marson

PART 4: TRANSFORMATION

Chapter 10: Noise? Shh! Happiness is here, now

There is enough information to awaken you to a new level of understanding and to consciously decide whether to boost your happiness. We will continue to build on this foundation in the next book.

To truly experience happiness, you must first become aware of the noise in your own life.

Where does the noise come from and how can you silence it?

To feel the happiness, the peace, the joy of being alive, you have to realize what distracts you, from the wonderful moments that you could experience, at any given time, in the first place. What distracts you from happiness?

Is it the TV?

_____

What shows/ programs/ movies give you a negative mood/ change your emotional state and take up your time every day?

_____

How can you stop this noise?

_____

Is it a radio station?

_____

What shows / programs / songs give you a negative mood / change your mood and take up your time every day?

_____

How can you stop this noise?

_____

Is it your phone?

_____

What activities on the phone take up your daily time/ generate a negative mood?

_____

How can you stop this noise?

_____

Learn to experience how liberating peace is.

Is there a specific app that you use, without stopping, just to waste time and feed your anxiety and the little monster, which says that you are not good enough?

_____

What makes it so attractive and why do you use it so often?

_____

How much time do you spend on this app, daily?

_____

What positive activities can you do instead to generate positive emotions?

_____

How can you stop this noise/ addiction?

_____

Are there any people around you who constantly criticize you, who constantly discourage you, who treat you in an unworthy way? Who? Be honest with yourself.

_____

What makes you allow such treatment?

_____

How can you stop this noise?

_____

For anything else, which adds to the noise in your life and, implicitly, to the perpetuation of a negative emotional state, go through the same questions and give the answer to the question:

"How can I stop this noise?"

Now that you know how to identify and how to stop the noise around, it's time to do something practical and see if everything I say in these pages really works.

We will do a simple exercise, christened by me "Collect Joy!", So that you FEEL GOOD NOW. We will raise your vibration and implicitly your level of consciousness, as you saw on the Map of Consciousness, to feel a little the taste of a life in which you choose to put your well-being first and think positively, deliberately.

I invite you to be open and try.

What do you have to lose if you don't try?

I'll tell you! An instant state of well-being.

Step 1. Take a pencil.
Step 2. Write here how you feel at the moment.

_____

Step 3. As soon as you finish reading this step, close your eyes, put your hand on your heart, take three deep breaths and remember a moment in your life when you were truly happy.

Feel, see, breathe and enjoy that moment as if you are reliving it now, once again.

You will realize that you are already feeling good, even though you have not even closed your eyes yet.

After taking this step, write here, what moment you remembered and how you felt, while you had your eyes closed.

_____

_____

_____

_____

_____

Step 4. As soon as you finish reading this step, close your eyes, put your hand on your heart, take three deep breaths and think of 3 things for which you are deeply grateful here and now.

Feel, see and breathe gratitude with all your heart, now and here, in the present moment.

You will realize that you are already feeling well again, even though you haven't even closed your eyes yet.

After taking this step, write here the 3 things you are deeply grateful for.

_____

_____

_____

_____

Step 5. As soon as you finish reading this step, close your eyes, put your hand on your heart, take three deep breaths and visualize how you are living an extraordinary moment, with someone you love, with all your being, somewhere in the future.

Feel, see, breathe and enjoy that moment, as if you are living it in reality.

You will realize that you are already feeling good again, even though you haven't even closed your eyes yet.

After taking this step, write here, what moment you imagined and how you felt while your eyes were closed.

_____

_____

_____

_____

_____

_____

_____

_____

Step 6. Write how you feel now.

_____

_____

_____

_____

_____

_____

_____

_____

What did you actually do?

You have just consciously directed your thoughts to the positive things in your life, to things that make you feel good instantly. You explored past, present and future.

Is it easy to feel good?

Yes / No

Is it a choice to feel good at all times?

Yes / No

Do people choose to feel good, consciously?

Yes / No

Do you want to feel good most of the time?

Yes / No

If you answered yes to the last question, I challenge you to do this exercise as many times as you want, invoking other memories and other people.

You can consciously choose to bathe in the memory of beautiful moments in the past, gratitude for the present, just as you can consciously choose to dream with open eyes the future you want to live.

No global pandemic, no news, no challenge can take this power away from you.

You choose what you want to think about, at any time.

Wake up more often to this truth and use it, every day, in your favor.

Wouldn't it be great to wake up every day feeling good?

Wouldn't it be great to wake up excited for the next day?

Wouldn't it be wonderful to think positive thoughts and be in a positive state from which you can consciously build the life you want to live, regardless of the dramas that are thrown in front of you?

Wouldn't it be great to be on a wave of happiness every day?

Wouldn't it be great to awaken to a new level of understanding every day?

Wouldn't it be great to remember every day that life is about having fun, enjoying every moment and feeling good?

If you have played this game 100% and you think it would be great to experience all this, every day, then it is my turn to tell you something you already know, somewhere in the depths of your being:

YOU ARE THE CHANGE YOU ARE WAITING FOR.

You can start by recognizing with detachment where you are now in your life and how you got here.

You can start by becoming aware of how you feel most of the time.

You can start by observing what thoughts go through your mind when you feel good and what thoughts go through your mind when you are not feeling well.

You can start by writing down the negative thoughts you notice, to get them out of your mind, where they run on autopilot and have them in front of your eyes, where you can decide what is true for you and what is not.

Every time you feel emotionally affected by what is happening around you or simply for no reason, I want you to ask yourself this:

What am I thinking at the moment?
Where does this thought come from?
Is this thought true?
What evidence do I have that this thought is true?
What better thoughts can I think of now?

Do not imagine that everything happens overnight and that you will stop all those tens of thousands of automatic thoughts instantly. Everything is a process, which you accelerate every time you become aware of how you feel and every time you ask yourself, what are the thoughts that cause you that state.

Sometimes, when I realize that I am emotionally affected by something, I send my mind to enjoy a day at the beach in Bali. I visualize myself enjoying the breeze, with a coconut cocktail in my hand, while the sun caresses my skin and the sound of the waves caresses my soul.

Suddenly, the agitated thoughts dissolve.

I feel so good even now as I type, just at the thought of this mental picture. Wait until I close my eyes. It gets better.

Other times, I express my gratitude because I am healthy, I have a wonderful family, friends I can count on, a goal so well lit in my heart.

Sometimes I dream with open eyes of the future I want. A future in which suffering no longer exists, a future in which people are good to each other, a future in which we are not waiting for someone else to change what does not suit us, a future in which we cooperate with each other in harmony and build a better future for the generations to come. How good and beautiful this feels!

Why does it work, every time?

Because the brain can't tell the difference between reality and what you imagine.

Imagine you are eating a lemon.

Do you taste the lemon? Can you feel the taste in your mouth? How can you do it? I did not give you a real lemon, I just asked you to imagine one. You see? You can hack your brain at any time, exactly the way you want.

Create your own paradise where you can escape, at least for a fresh mouth of hope, every time the environment turns into a source of stress, sadness, mental exhaustion.

 Try this:

Every time I feel overwhelmed by a negative situation, I will remember that I have the power to control how I feel, by controlling where I give my attention and energy and I will travel mentally here. Be as specific as possible:

_____

_____

_____

_____

_____

_____

The reason you suffer, when you create dramatic scenarios in your mind and you are in a loop of negative thinking, is because your brain does NOT differentiate between what you imagine and reality. Wouldn't it be great to use this to your advantage and create positive scenarios?

Your brain interprets what you see and what you think, whether fiction or reality, as reality.

That's why you cry when you watch drama movies or you're still terrified even a few days, since you saw a horror movie. Your brain is stronger than you think, so be careful what you feed it with daily.

You are the creator of your reality and you create this reality with the power of your mind.

You have the power to choose, at any time of the day, how you want to feel.

All you need in order for you to start creating your own reality is a decision to do so. And a lot of practice. And patience.

At first you won't see too many differences.

Over time, however, you will become better and better at tracking, controlling and choosing your thoughts deliberately. The great part is that when you get there, you will be able to stay more and more in a continuous state of good, peace, happiness.

I promise you that after a little effort, an extraordinary reward awaits you and that when you are a master at controlling your thoughts, the way you will feel at any time of the day will make you never want to you let your thoughts wander, automatically, through your mind, as they once did. Perseverance and consistency will change your life.

It all starts with the decision to take the helm of your happiness.

"If you don't learn how to control your thoughts, you'll never learn how to control your behavior."

- Joyce Mayer

To tempt you to feel better and better and to be happier every day, I have prepared a super simple challenge with immediate implementation.

Here's what you need to do.

EVERY EVENING, BEFORE SLEEPING

Set your intention to wake up with a smile on your face. That's it. It is easy to do it and the huge impact it has, in the long run, is measured on your own skin. You will regain your enthusiasm for being alive.

It's worth a try.

"Intention gives you direction."

- **Cristina Joy**

EVERY MORNING, AS SOON AS YOU WAKE UP

1. Notice how you feel when the first thing you do when you wake up is smile.

Your smile sends a signal to your brain that everything is fine and even though you just opened your eyes, you start the day in a positive tone. If you want to take this step to the next level, smile looking into your eyes, in the mirror, and give yourself a Hi5. Don't take my word for it! Test what I say.

2. Ask yourself:

How do I want to feel today? And choose, as from a catalog of happiness, whatever you want. The good part? Any choice is free.

Ex: happy, full of energy, cheerful, smiling, focused, productive, playful, creative, determined, curious, disciplined, good, kind, loving.

If you do this: you set an intention and you are proactive. You decide that whatever happens in your day, you will be as you set out to be.

If you don't do this: you are reactive and you become the victim of what happens in your day. If the day goes well, you'll be fine. If the day doesn't go too well, you won't be fine.

I am convinced that you know people who always say, when you ask them how their day is going:

"Right now I'm good. Let's see what's going to happen next!"

This is a typical response for environmental victims. They respond as if, they are surprised that they feel ok and that everything is ok and they feel that this will not last long, that something will happen and they will have to react and get out of the state of well-being.

3. The mirror of the soul. The next level in this practice is to use a mirror and look into your own eyes while answering the question on how you want to feel today.

I use the mirror version, I look into my eyes and, what I noticed is that, as I repeat this practice, I start to develop an ever better relationship with the person in the mirror.

Such a practice really matters a lot, as we have been taught how to behave with those around us, but never how to behave with ourselves. We were taught how to encourage other people, but never how to encourage ourselves. We were educated how to build relationships with those around us, but not with ourselves.

Using the mirror will give you a huge boost of self-confidence.

Here's how I answer my question about how I want to feel today:

I adopt a huge smile and look into my eyes, in the mirror.

I give myself a Hi5 in the mirror, as if I'm extremely happy to see my best friend and I tell myself with wonderful energy and enthusiasm:

"Today I will feel intuitive.
Today I will feel inspired.
Today I will feel connected.
Today I will be full of energy.
Today I will feel alive and full of life.
Today I will feel happy.
Today I will feel confident in my strength.
Today I will feel brave.
Today I will be aware of how I feel.
Today I will be aware of my thoughts.
Today I will be full of joy.
Today I will be playful.
Today I will emanate love.
Today I will have fun.
Today I will be creative.
I will be active today.
Today I will be disciplined.
Today I will be kind to myself and those around me.
Today I will be calm.
Today I will be in the best shape.
Today I will enjoy the present moment.
I will make today count. "

If you want some more examples to recharge your batteries:

"I will be innovative today.
Today I will feel invigorated.
Today I will be inspired in every moment.
Today I will have only wonderful interactions.
Today I will feel that I deserve the best.
Today I will prove that I deserve the best, through the happiness I emanate.
Today I feel it's my right to feel good.
I am unconditionally happy.
I feel good and I know that everything is in my favor.
I am blessed at every moment of the day.
Today I will learn a lot of new things.
Today I will evolve as a person. "

Tell yourself these statements every morning and BOOM! Notice how you feel! Repeat during the day.
Now you know how to set yourself up for an extraordinary day and you know how to set yourself up to enjoy every moment, no matter what happens around you.
You can only save the world after you save yourself first. You can spread happiness only after you become happy.

GET READY FOR THE UNEXPECTED
The unforeseen is part of life. If you ask me, the unforeseen really gives flavor to this human experience.
I challenge you to make a list of 10 things that don't cost money and that instantly bring a smile to your face and the

joy of being alive. Use it every time the unexpected happens and you need to get back on the waterline quickly.

10 THINGS THAT BRING ME HAPPINESS:

1. _____
2. _____
3. _____
4. _____
5. _____
6. _____
7. _____
8. _____
9. _____
10 . _____

I must admit that I have a list of more than ten, with the simplest things possible. A sunrise, a sunset, a barefoot walk through the grass, a smile, a random act of kindness, a clear sky, the sound of waves, a child's laughter, a warm hug, the breeze felt on the cheeks...

Is it important to constantly remember what makes you truly happy? Don't you deserve to enjoy this experience called life to the fullest?

Isn't this life too short to live other than happy, full of energy, cheerful, enthusiastic?

This book is one of the most wonderful gifts you could give yourself.

Now that you've done your part and reached the end of it, play with me a little more. After reading the steps:

1. Close your eyes.
2. Take three deep breaths.
3. Imagine that you have yourself in front of you.

4. Smile at the person in front of you with all possible love and sincerity.

5. See how the person in front of you shakes off all the dust and all the limitations and challenges experienced so far.

6. Tell him/ her how proud you are of yourself.

7. Now give yourself the strongest hug you can give.

8. Feel the connection with yourself, remembering that your brain will feel the whole experience as real, and this will make you feel connected, encouraged and loved by yourself.

You can use this visualization whenever you need encouragement, a boost of courage, feel alone. WE END WITH AN INSTANT HAPPINESS BOOST, ANNULATOR OF FEAR, ANXIETY, DEPRESSION:

PRACTICE GRATITUDE DAILY

Write 5 things a day that you are grateful for.
Start today. I am grateful for:

1. _____

2. _____

3. _____

4. _____

5. _____

Feel them, live them, be truly grateful.

What do I want you to remember? At least one idea:

YOUR LIFE CAN BE A PRISON OR AN EXTRAORDINARY ADVENTURE!

You can be the victim or the creator of your life.

It all depends on what you choose to think about it.

You have my deepest appreciation and pure love because you chose to go through these lines and connect with my energy and thoughts.

All I have to say is thank you from the bottom of my heart for allowing me to reach to you, regardless of the space and time that separates us, and to offer you my sincere friendship and my pure thought, through which I wish you to blessed with love, happiness and a life full of joy as a result of intersecting with this message.

Awaken Yourself. Book 1, from the series of 7 books.

May the Universe align our paths in

Awaken Yourself. Book 2, 11 Secrets of Evolved Relationships, in which we will continue what we have begun to build here.

"We are all connected. With each other, biological.
With the Earth, chemically.
With the whole universe, at the atomic level.
Not only are we in the Universe,
The universe is in US. "

- Neil deGrasse Tyson

If you feel that this book has helped you in any way and you feel that other souls could be helped by it too, I encourage you to borrow it, give it away or recommend it.
This world needs as many happy people as possible.
Consciously choose to be one of them.
See you soon, dear soul!
Thank you, Cristina Joy

About the Author

© Cristina Joy

Cristina Joy is a passionate writer, International Trainer, Transformational Coach and Human Spirit Developer, based in London and totally in love with humanity. Cristina is on a mission to stop human suffering, to help, to inspire and to spread joy to every soul with which she intersects her path.

She is an extremely smiling, energetic and positive being, who shares her feel-good vibe, instantly.

She aspires to spread her message to millions of people globally, and until then, she modestly enjoys her humble beginning.

Cristina wants you to read this book with your soul and not with your mind. This is the only way you will be able to embrace her authentic and imperfect style.

Cristina is deeply grateful for the courage with which she began this journey, while she happily continues her evolution through life, inspiring others, along the way, to do the same.

Cristina honors the opportunity to remind you that we are all perfect in our imperfection and that, in the end, we are just walking each other home.

Acknowledgments

A huge "Thank you!" to all those who contributed directly or indirectly to the publication of this book.

Thank you with love and gratitude mom and dad, thanks to you this stubborn and full of joy soul is here.

 Without you, this book would not have existed.

Somehow, everything happens in a natural order.

I have a huge gratitude for all the people in my life. Those who have been, those who are and those who will be.

I have learned, I am learning and I will learn, constantly, from everyone.

My heartfelt thanks to my family and best friends who have become my family.

Another huge "Thank You" goes to all the teachers in the path of my life, people who, through shared experiences, pushed me forward, on the scale of my evolution, even when I did not want to move a millimeter.

A deep "Thank you" with love and gratitude to the most important mentors on my journey to awakening:

Jim Rohn, David R. Hawkins, Dr. Joe Dispenza, Tony Robbins, T. Harv Eker, Jay Shetty, John Bradshaw, Neale Donald Walsh, Esther / Abraham and Jerry Hicks, Deepak Chopra, Brendon Buchard, Sadhguru, Robin Norwood, John Gottman, John Gray, James Clear.

I have to say a huge "Thank you" to this stubborn soul who resides within me and who inspired me to write this book with clarity at turbo speed, so that I can publish it, with courage, on 11/11/2020 at 11:11.

In the end, I thank most true and unpredictable mentor, **LIFE.**

Discover the 11 secrets of evolved relationships in Awaken Yourself Book 2

Thank you from the bottom of my heart, stubborn soul,
for wanting to enjoy life more, for embracing insecurity
and for throwing yourself headlong into the unknown.
I love you. I honor you. I appreciate you.
We are connected.
Until the next book, stay blessed!

Send me your thoughts:
cristina@joyacademyglobal.com
www.joyacademyglobal.com

CONTENTS

Printed in Great Britain
by Amazon